On All Cylinders

On All Cylinders

The Entrepreneur's Handbook

Ron Robinson

BEP BUSINESS EXPERT PRESS

On all Cylinders: The Entrepreneur's Handbook
Copyright © Business Expert Press, LLC, 2016.

First published in 2016 by
Business Expert Press, LLC
222 East 46th Street, New York, NY 10017
www.businessexpertpress.com

ISBN-13: 978-1-63157-556-3 (paperback)
ISBN-13: 978-1-63157-557-0 (e-book)

Business Expert Press Human Resource Management and Organizational Behavior Collection

Collection ISSN: 1946-5637 (print)
Collection ISSN: 1946-5645 (electronic)

Cover and interior design by S4Carlisle Publishing Services Private Ltd., Chennai, India

First edition: 2016

10 9 8 7 6 5 4 3 2 1

Printed in the United States of America.

Dedication

This book is dedicated to all the management teams I have served over 40 years and to my wife Judy who patiently and conscientiously reviewed every page of this book and encouraged me to continue.

Abstract

I continually hear business owners and leaders express frustration with their personnel. There is not one organization I work with that first, has an aligned strategy; second, communicates well, has effective meetings, consistently makes informed decisions; third, works with people collaboratively; fourth, motivates with more than an occasional pat on the back and fifth, effectively innovates new products or services. Yet these elements can make or break a business.

Most small and mid sized businesses that survived the Great Recession offer limited management training, not to mention leadership development. Entrepreneurs are so busy that any leadership development is through the Graduate School of Hard Knocks. The business community is being inundated with shifting market demands along with a wider mix of generations and cultures. Millennials, many of whom are proud of their technical skills and themselves, combined with Gen Xers who are eagerly anticipating management responsibilities and Baby Boomers who expect to be appreciated for their knowledge and experience, present dilemmas for many organizations today. As one executive put it, "Diverse cultures are no problem, it is generational differences that take most of my time. Millennials expect everything to be done quickly and Baby Boomers expect others to do things their way."

I have learned that no matter what differences exist in the workplace, there are values everyone tends to share. Fair play, being heard, being in the know, being recognized for good work, equal opportunity to excel and being shown respect are important to everyone.

This book has been written to address 21st Century challenges of rapidly shifting market demands along with generational differences. It is designed to integrate those values within a system of leadership behaviors that develop collaborative and creative cultures. It can be pulled off the shelf or pulled up on an app to solve a particular problem. Or, it can be used to enable any leadership team apply all the system's components and unleash the hidden power in their organization, respond rapidly to market changes and achieve greater business success. The choice is theirs!

Keywords

21st Century Leadership, Balanced Scorecards, Collaboration, Communication, Culture, Customer Satisfaction, Employee Satisfaction, Global Leadership, Innovation, Management, Motivation, New Normal, Productivity, Profits, Project Management, Quick Response to Change, Strategic Alignment, World Class Leaders

Contents

Introduction

The attacks of 9'11 and The Great Recession affected us all and created a new economy in the process. The result has been greater demands for management to unleash the power within diverse workforces and rapidly respond to market and technology changes.

These changes require managers to become 21st Century leaders in which their total organization is on the same page, pulling in the same direction supporting the mission and highly aware of customer demands.

Their new roles include moving communication with speed and accuracy and having high ethical standards. They create an environment in which everyone feels like owners in the business and performs at a higher level. Leaders must become fantastic listeners in which everyone is discussing how to make operations and products better and making informed decisions. Instead of good ideas being lost, the leader has them packaged in a project plan and implemented. As a result, operations respond faster to market and technology changes in this New Normal economy.

Today's workplaces consist of greater cultural and generational diversity providing challenges for most management teams. Millennials, many of whom are proud of their technical skills and themselves, combined with GenXers who are eagerly anticipating management responsibilities and Baby Boomers who expect to be appreciated for their knowledge and experience, present dilemmas for many organizations today. As one executive put it, "Diverse cultures are no problem, it is generational differences that take most of my time. Millennials expect everything to be done quickly and Baby Boomers expect others to do things their way."

In order to manage workplace differences and resolve resulting conflicts many businesses provide diversity training. There are a number of diversity strategies available for clients and extensive studies of generational differences have been conducted. The studies tend to characterize Traditionals being born before 1945, Baby Boomers born after 1945, Generation Xers born after 1965 and Millennials born after 1977.

According to Psychologist, Constance Patterson, PhD, Training Director for Louisiana School Psychology Internship Consortium, there are several characteristics worth noting.

"Gen Xers seem to be focused more on themselves and moving up the organizational ladder rapidly. Their loyalty appears to be more to themselves than their employers.

Baby Boomers may see Gen Xers as impatient and eager to challenge the status quo.

Traditional may perceive Boomers as thinking they have all the answers and are unwilling to listen to others.

All generations may see Traditionals as controlling and dictatorial, Gen Xers may see Millennials as having strong egos and Millennials may consider Gen Xers as being sour and negative."

Patterson notes that teamwork provides a method for all generations to work together and collaborate. She offers the following suggestions for each generation:

"Traditionals need to hear, "Your experience is respected or "It is valuable to hear what has worked in the past." Baby Boomers need to hear such messages as, "You are valuable, worthy", or "Your contribution is important for our success.' Gen Xers may need to hear, "Let's explore options out of the box" or "Your technical expertise is a big asset."

Millennials may seek similar messages like, "You will be collaborating with other bright, creative people" or "You have really rescued this situation with your commitment."

I have learned that no matter what differences exist in the workplace there are several values everyone shares: fair play, being heard, being in the know, being recognized for good work, equal opportunity to progress, and being shown respect.

My goal is to integrate those values within a system of leadership behaviors to assist you developing collaborative and creative cultures within your diverse workplaces.

As the pace of change accelerates, organizations must respond faster than ever before. Business leaders can make the changes work for them by using their unique strengths to make their diverse organizations better, and in the process, create greater wealth for their businesses, employees and communities.

Most small and mid-sized businesses that survived the Great Recession offer limited management training, not to mention leadership development. Entrepreneurs are so busy that any leadership development is through the Graduate School of Hard Knocks. I continually hear business owners and management express frustration with their ability to accomplish goals with their personnel. Yet there is not one organization I serve that first, has an aligned strategy; second, communicates well; third, works with people collaboratively and makes informed decisions; fourth, motivates with more than an occasional pat on the back; and fifth, effectively innovates new products or services. These elements can make or break a business in this 21st century economy.

I would like to thank a colleague of mine who encouraged me to write this book. He mentioned that it is very hard to find good people to work in his business. After several discussions, we realized it might be a leadership issue rather than an insufficient supply of qualified candidates. I realized there are a lot of good people in business who would have an interest in learning how managers can become leaders making a difference in the 21st century. Furthermore, in order for today's leaders to process information they demand something they can take off the shelf and use. This book is unique in that it provides time tested tools that can be easily applied to improve performance, create a collaborative culture, and maintain a competitive business.

This book has been 40 years in the making. I have been both an executive and consultant helping organizations around the world become more competitive in their marketplaces.

I am trained and certified in performance management, lean organization design, process improvement, total quality management using high performing work teams, strategy development, mediation, leadership coaching, and leadership course development. I have coached leaders from CEO's and other corporate executives to managers, supervisors and key personnel in fortune 500's, non-profits, and governmental agencies in order for them to work more effectively with their personnel to improve operational performance.

For 10 years, I served as Human resource Deputy for a software development company with responsibility for benefit administration, salary administration, executive and IT recruiting, and leadership development. Other industries I served as a consultant include Healthcare, Information Technology, Manufacturing, Transportation, Hospitality, Quick Service Restaurants, Public Service operations, Nonprofits, and Small Businesses.

I was born and raised in a small mountain town, Tazewell, Virginia. Tazewell's population was 4,000 if you count a dog or two. While Tazewell was much smaller than surrounding towns, it managed to have superior elementary and high school programs with high levels of scholastic achievement along with dominating football and basketball teams. Years later, I talked to someone in a nearby town who commented on the dominance of our football teams. How could a town so small dominate schools much larger having greater resources? It was the system used by Tazewell. From the time I was 8 years old I played football.

Pewee, Junior Varsity and Varsity teams all practiced using the same plays. By the time I was ready for varsity ball, I knew by heart the basic plays our team would run. That was how Tazewell's football coach maintained dominance. The school had a system and formula for winning and maintained that system for years. Each person on our team knew well from practice, summer camps, and repetition what was required of every player to win.

That concept also applies to business management and developing winning and dominant organizations. This book is designed to provide you with a system and formula for developing creative and innovative organizational behavior. The book is organized into concepts that when used together can be a winning combination and when used separately bring incremental change requiring more time to accomplish your goals. The choice will be yours and yours alone.

It has been my experience that organizations who educate all leaders together from the executive suite to first line supervision, successfully transform their culture, and pull people together to win in today's competitive markets. I have seen organizations over the years perform better and quicker and believe you can do the same by using the skills and processes offered in the following chapters.

CHAPTER 1

Leadership System

"If leaders expect staff to meet and exceed the expectations of their customers, those same leaders must respond to concerns and exceed expectations on behalf of their staff."

—Joseph A. Michelli,
The Starbucks Experience

Traditional Management

We are provided leadership skills through life experiences both at home and at work. In addition, certain personality styles lend themselves to qualities of leadership that assist in your leadership journey. In this chapter, you will learn a leadership system used by successful leaders that can assist you advance your skill set. I can remember as a child telling myself that I would never say to my children some of the things my father said to me. However, when I became a father I heard some of the same phrases coming out of my mouth! You may have similar experiences.

Just as we are shaped by our parents, we are shaped by supervisors and managers who guide us as we begin our professional careers. That is why it is important to think of leadership as a system of behaviors that can be learned and applied in everyday situations at work and at home. The good news is that there may be certain behaviors to master in today's world of work but we have learned many of them along the way. We need to focus only on a critical few in order to have the total skill set required for pulling everyone together and moving your organizations into the future.

The traditional leadership system was created from a military tradition. For decades, organizations have experienced success using the system shown in Figure 1.1.

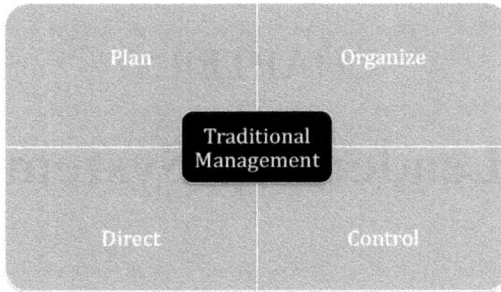

Figure 1.1 Traditional model

In this system, managers are taught to plan and organize work for their employees and operations. They learn to execute plans by directing and following up with each person in their sphere of control to ensure that work is performed accurately and on time. Employees are expected to be good listeners and perform as directed.

21st-Century Leadership

In today's environment of diverse cultures represented by multiple generations, a new form of management system is required. Organizations are being challenged to create a culture of pluralism that is collaborative and innovative to compete in today's marketplace.

The manner in which behaviors are organized into a system of leadership develops a common culture when used organization wide. That system consists of the five circles shown in Figure 1.2, illustrating Alignment,

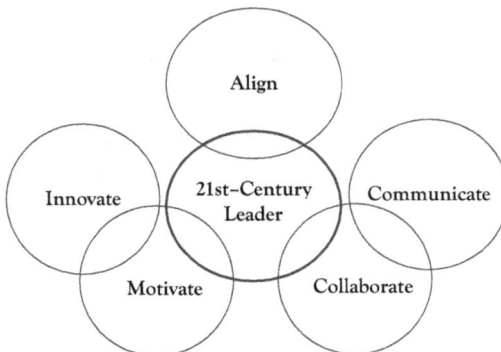

Figure 1.2 21st Century leadership model

Communication, Collaboration, Motivation, and Innovation. This book will review each element of the system and accompanying behaviors integral for your organization becoming the best in your marketplace. Figure 1.2 illustrates how you can lead your organization to think out of the box.

Leadership System

Alignment means the personnel in your organization know the direction of the company, its goals, teams' goals, and how each supports the other. It means having data and scorecards that inform all staff of the progress toward goal achievement and making improvements. It means everyone in the organization can recite the vision, mission, and principles of your organization. *The leadership behaviors that contribute to alignment include developing and sharing vision and strategy, planning and organizing around strategy, and linking associates with customers and strategy.*

Communication means having the information needed to perform each person's duties and accomplish their goals. It includes regularly scheduled meetings in which scorecards and plans are updated and everyone shares their activities and what they have learned. It also includes the use of technology to instantly update persons and teams with information to help them optimize their talents and accomplish their tasks and goals. Communication involves the *leadership behaviors of listening before speaking, meeting regularly with staff, building trust, and modeling ethical behavior.*

Collaboration means that the organization is organized into a team system in which each team's members meet regularly to discuss ideas for solving problems and improvement in the way work is performed, products and services are enhanced, and new products and services are designed. Customer requirements are part of any discussion regarding work improvements as well as product and service enhancements and new product design. The team's ideas are utilized, thus creating an innovative workplace. *Collaboration relies on leadership behaviors of driving out fear, facilitating, encouraging new ideas, and delegating.*

Motivation means there are both short and long-term rewards and recognition for accomplishments. They are contingent on improvements in organizational scorecards and goal attainment and can range from short-term incentives such as time off to long-term stock owner-ship plans. It means the culture has four times more positive feedback than corrective feedback. *Leadership behaviors required for motivating the workforce include understanding human behavior, celebrating improvements and goal attainment, positive thinking, calmly correcting behavior, and being flexible in leadership styles with associates.*

Innovation means the organization has created a culture in which people feel free to express themselves and are encouraged to think out

TRADITIONAL MANAGEMENT	21ST-CENTURY LEADER
Plan and Organize	**Align**
Undefined vision or strategy	Develops vision, principles, and strategy with staff
Work plans assigned to staff	Plans and organizes tasks with staff
Focuses on production	Links team with customers
Direct	**Communicate**
Speaks over others	Listens before speaking
Meets with individual staff members	Meets regularly with staff as a unit
End justifies the means	Lives by principles
Distrust	Builds trust
Control	**Collaborate**
Finds blame	Drives out fear and gives credit
Dictates	Facilitates
Provides solutions	Encourages creativity
Makes decisions	Delegates decisions
Manage by Exception	**Motivate**
Criticizes	Celebrates
Avoids risk	Encourages problem solving
Corrects loudly and publicly	Corrects calmly and privately
Staff conforms to leaders' style	Leader adapts to individual and group styles
Statis Quo	**Innovative**
Standards	Principles
Individual contribution	Team creation
Compete	Play
Inform as need to know	Protect confidences as unit

Figure 1.3 Behavior shift

of the box and create ways to reduce costs, improve productivity, quality, product performance, new products and services and organizational designs for future growth. The culture is created using behaviors defined earlier and aligned within the five circles. In addition, the following behaviors are used *when creating a new product or service: Follow Principles of Innovation, Create Project Team, Encourage Purposeful Play, and Maintain Confidences.*

Figure 1.3 illustrates behavior changes required to shift from a traditional culture to a collaborative and innovative culture.

ALIGNMENT

"First, have a definite, clear practical ideal; a goal, an objective. Second, have the necessary means to achieve your ends; wisdom, money, materials, and methods. Third, adjust all your means to that end."

—Aristotle

CHAPTER 2

Balanced Strategy

The ability to align the people in your operation with the goals of the enterprise is a critical part of leadership. Alignment includes the behaviors of a leader who facilitates the development of a vision and principles with a balanced strategy and goals with the team, develops a balanced scorecard to track progress, and organizes staff and tasks to best accomplish goals. A critical element of innovation involves inclusion of customers and other stakeholders with your team members when developing your strategy. The purpose is to ensure team members are completely aligned with their customers and your organization's plan. At the very least, stakeholders to invite to the planning session should include key customers and suppliers.

A paper manufacturing operation went through a two-day process to identify their vision and mission with supporting principles. Their work was posted just inside the main entrance of headquarters. The executives found that many potential clients converted to new clients after visiting and learning how this supplier aligned with their values. The process for creating a living strategy aligned with your workforce is shown in Figure 2.1.

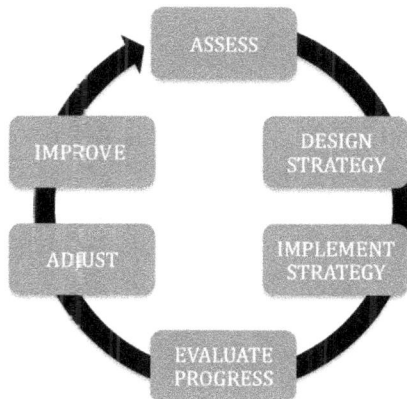

Figure 2.1 Strategy development process

A balanced strategy includes a vision for the future, a mission for accomplishing the vision, principles defining ethical behavior and goals, and tasks identified for accomplishing the vision and mission. For example:

Our vision is to lead our industry. Our mission is to continually innovate through a process of Discovery, Designing Solutions, Implementing Solutions, Evaluating Results, and Continually Improving.

Our Principles:

1. Tell the Truth First, Last, Always
2. Do Right
3. Collaborate and Innovate
4. Open Communication
5. Teamwork at Every Level
6. Continually and Relentlessly Improve
7. Feedback
8. Fact-based Decision Making
9. Transparency
10. Encourage Risk
11. Have Fun

The key elements of strategic goal development involve consideration of the four pillars of an organization including Financials, Operations, Customers, and Employees (Figure 2.2).

Financials include both revenue and expense goals with tasks defined to accomplish those goals. Many organizations believe their task is complete with a set of financial goals and objectives for the year. Nothing could be further from the truth. Such an organization will have good profit margins while operations become obsolete, employees become less skilled, and customers change suppliers. Operational goals could include new or improved equipment, technology changes, and supplier relationships as examples. Customer goals have to do with increasing customer counts, analyzing customers' purchasing habits and developing new clients while retaining desired existing customers. Employee goals are

Finance   Operations   Employee Sat   Customer Sat

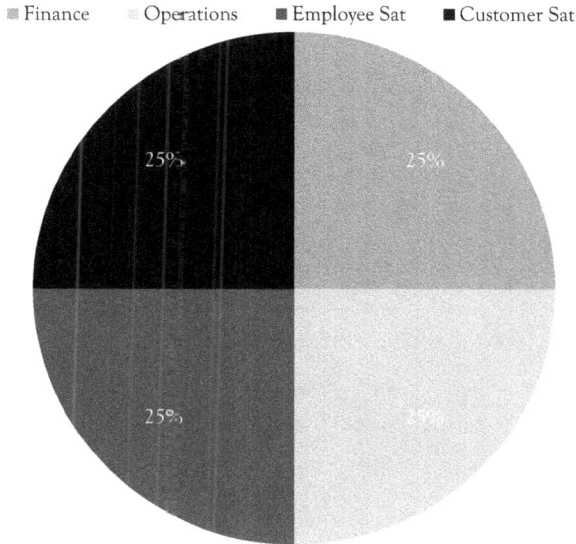

Figure 2.2 Balance illustration

typically focused on enhancing employee performance, reducing turn-over, enhancing skill sets, and recruitment of new talent.

Organizations focusing solely on their financials find the result to be discontented employees and inefficient operations. They may reduce costs but typically lose market share in the process.

Just as misdirected is the organization focusing solely on customers. It may experience market gains but be unable to remain competitive because of poorly maintained operations and low margins. It takes focus on core components of the organization (its four pillars) in order to increase innovation and competitiveness in today's marketplace.

If your strategy does not consider operations with goals for change or improvement, customers with goals for retaining current customers, and attracting new customers and goals for retaining and improving performance of your human capital, then your organization will have little chance to innovate and sustain itself through the 21st Century.

The process for developing an innovative strategy includes assessing the present state of the organization through discovery. Learning the needs and perspective of an organization's customers is critical before developing a strategy for serving them. Learning the needs and issues of staff is important in order to best serve the needs of customers in your

Service	Rating 1=Poor 5=Exceeds	Change	Keep
Emergency room	4	Uncomfortable seating	Nice personnel
Outpatient	3	Long waits to 20 minutes or less	Quality care
Behavioral health	1	24-hour on-site mental health provider	N/A
Billing	2	Simplify and provide costs before treatment	N/A

Figure 2.3 Product/service evaluation tool

market place. Considering associates to be part of your customer base and a key link in your customer chain helps when developing your plan of action.

An example of an assessment tool is shown in Figure 2.3. Using this tool, customers are interviewed to identify the products and services used by them. They are then asked to evaluate satisfaction with each item and to offer solutions for improvement. The recommendations are included when developing the strategic plan.

Survey Guidelines

1. The unit's employees and customers should be involved and together during the interview process. The process enhances the relationship and communication between suppliers and customers.
2. Unit employees should listen to customer comments and avoid explaining away concerns expressed by customers. If employees defend their actions, customers will become discouraged and simply tell the unit what they want to hear. The only time employees should speak is to ask questions and rephrase customer comments.
3. At the end of the interview, employees should thank customers for their honesty, feedback, and willingness to assist them perform better.
4. When developing a vision and strategy for the organization ratings and recommendations from the survey, results can be used to create goals and tactics for Customer Satisfaction, Financial Management, Employee Satisfaction, and Operational Performance.

Financial Goals	Operation Goals	Customer Goals	Employee Goals
Goal: Increase sales by 10% Tactic: Release one gizmo in Q2 and another in Q4 Tactic: Hire two representatives for new releases	Goal: Reduce cycle time by 20% Tactic: Implement Six Sigma and total quality management Tactic: Research robotics and make recommendation Tactic: Introduce digital tablets for all employees	Goal: Exceed market expectations Tactic: Design survey and schedule visits with all key clients Tactic: Organize two cross functional teams and visit a broad sample of clients to determine next generation of product offerings	Goal: Increase employee satisfaction scores to 98% Tactic: Organize an Employee Sat team to communicate and implement survey findings Tactic: Train all managers based on findings Tactic: Distribute and train everyone to use new tablets

Figure 2.4 Balanced strategy example

After assessment data are collected and summarized, the strategy is developed with an action plan for implementation. During implementation, it is important to regularly and consistently evaluate progress toward goal attainment and make adjustments. The following year the process begins again.

Successful organizations have such a process. Before strategic planning, the leadership team will visit competitor's operations to discover their strong points and potential weaknesses. They assess customer sentiment. They evaluate their own operations to discover gaps between their competitors, their customers, and themselves. When planning, marketing staff and customers are included to ensure their innovation strategy addresses current and future needs of their market. Members of staff and front line employees also participate during planning and goal development. An example of a balanced strategy is shown in Figure 2.4

Balanced Scorecard for an Aligned Workplace

A balanced scorecard is typically a set of graphs and charts updating progress toward established goals. The purpose of a balanced scorecard is to align strategic goals with all employees in the organization. By visualizing progress toward goal achievement, all staff are clearly focused when solving problems, removing barriers, innovating work and product

performance, creating new products and/or services, and celebrating successes. To maximize effectiveness, scorecards report baseline data and
goals and are frequently updated (weekly and monthly). The examples are
shown in Figures 2.5–2.8.

Figure 2.5 Finance *(Sales/Revenue)*

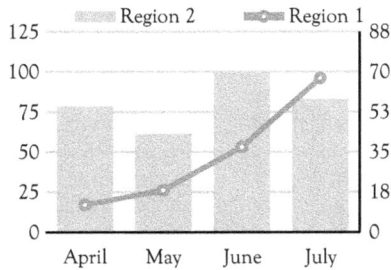

Figure 2.6 Operations *(SixSig, Robot, HndHld)*

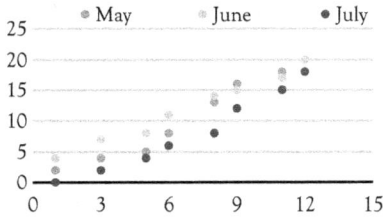

Figure 2.7 Employee satisfaction

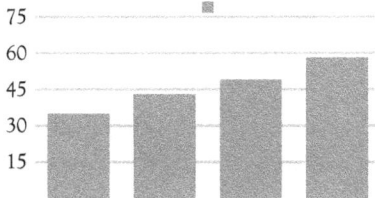

Figure 2.8 Customer satisfaction

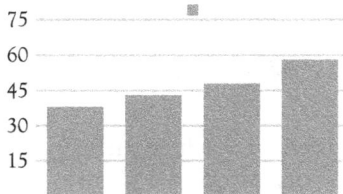

The data for Employee Satisfaction track with data for Customer Satisfaction. Research repeatedly shows a direct correlation between Employee Satisfaction and Customer Satisfaction. When Employee Satisfaction improves, so does Customer Satisfaction. It is also true that if employees are in conflict or otherwise dissatisfied and lack the resources to perform their duties, Customer Satisfaction data will drop as well.

You may notice the data graphed in Finance, Employee Satisfaction, and Customer Satisfaction are *outcome data* resulting from implementing the tactics of your strategy. The Operations scorecard tracks *process data* including the number of Six Sigma projects, number of hand held devices, and number of robotic devices installed in operations. Outcome data reflect the results of our activities while process data count the tasks we perform to deliver the outcomes we have defined.

Any sports coach I have known, including my own experience as a coach, develops a strategy for the season based on available talent and nature of teams in the conference. Every coach has measures of team performance as well as how each player performs on shots taken, shot blocks, steals, turnovers, assists, and so on. Without good data, team members have little chance to improve. One team I coached could not rebound missed shots. I began counting every time someone blocked out an opponent and caught rebounds. At every break in the game, players would come over to see how many block outs and rebounds they achieved. Within weeks, rebounding improved and we became competitive in our league.

As with sports, the same applies in business. A corporation, small business, or nonprofit requires data to evaluate performance. Imagine attending a basketball game and never knowing the score or number of fouls made. How long would you stay at the game, how many games would you attend without a scoreboard or method to measure winners and losers? It is no different with your business. Knowing the score makes a major difference in a leader and her team's ability to make decisions, keep the workforce aligned and focused, and remain dominant in her market.

Several factors are important to consider when developing a balanced scorecard or dashboard.

1. Charts should be regularly and consistently updated.

Many organizations want to measure monthly or quarterly. It is important to measure weekly instead. The reason is simple. By measuring the progress weekly, your team has a much better chance to make corrections in work in order to better meet monthly goals. Measuring monthly does not provide the information required for making mid-course corrections and is much less motivating to staff.

2. Charts should be prominently posted in a highly visible area of the workplace.

The reason for prominent display is to keep the focus of the operation "top of mind" with everyone. This is continuous alignment. Clear communication is important, and highly visible charts updated weekly is a proven way to provide relevant and helpful information to everyone in your operation.

3. Charts should be maintained and updated by staff.

If management maintains the graphs and charts, management will pay attention to them. If staff keeps the charts up to date, staff will pay attention to them.

4. Charts should be colorful and easily accessible.

Dull pictures tend to be ignored, and graphs can be ignored as well. Provide lots of color that tells the story. For example, a red line for your goal, green and blue lines for data, and black lines make graphs colorful and tell a story.

5. Charts should have goals.

Alignment of your workforce includes depicting the goals of the team or organization on the graphs. These goals align with company strategy goals. Each part of the organization can track progress, solve problems, and innovate when goals are not achieved.

6. Charts should be easily understood and easy to read.

A person new to your organization, including customers, should be able to glance at your graphs and know immediately how you are performing. Two companies I served worked diligently to have graphs posted that readily told the story of their focus and progress.

7. Charts should include baseline data to illustrate past performance.

Baseline data are collected and charted showing performance before you began implementing your strategy. Drawing a line at the point you begin making changes will help you evaluate progress versus past performance.

8. The organization's vision, mission, and principles should be posted with scorecards.

Ensure that everyone can describe how they are living the values in their workplace. A General Manager of a prominent hotel chain presented to our group when we were benchmarking companies. He pulled from his pocket a list of values. Every day he picks one value and visits his departments asking staff to recite the value of the day. Everyone is aligned with the values of that organization. And customers are delighted. And business is very good!

9. Data should be charted going up.

There is just something about the way we are wired. We like to see data go up in sports such as basketball, soccer, football, and so on, with exceptions of golf and track. It is the same in business. We like to see sales, quality productivity go up. And we like to see our graphs go up. So, if you are measuring errors, graph accuracy instead. If you are trying to improve absenteeism, graph attendance. Remember positive thinking for leaders. Good time to use it!!

The value of not only having a balanced set of measures but also implementing the concept throughout your organization cannot be emphasized enough. A manufacturing operation would annually invite us back to facilitate the planning exercise and then work on each shift to facilitate shift teams in deciding on measures to align with their plant's strategy. Each year the operation's performance improved over the past year, in part, because every person in the company knew their score weekly and monthly.

CHAPTER 3

Organized Staff

Earlier we discussed the importance of including staff when developing your strategy for your organization. It is just as important to include your staff when deciding how best to organize your program, assign tasks, and delegate decisions. They are the "world's greatest experts" when it comes to their own work and will have invaluable information to share regarding planning and organizational decisions. Planning involves annual updates of strategy, and organizing is the process of aligning your talent with the goals of the strategy for best results.

There are two options for organizing staff to accomplish program goals. The more traditional way identifies which individuals can best perform given tasks. For example, the leader assigns a mechanical engineer for robotic design, an industrial engineer to determine best production process, and an electrical engineer to design the digital requirements of the product. Production personnel are later assigned to produce robots.

Typically, each person will be given a list of tasks with a goal for task completion. Such an organization of individual task assignment and accountability was how I was managed for much of my career. I know other professionals who work in virtual isolation and are unaware of other personnel and tasks being completed.

As a leader I found a different design worked much better for my department and as a consultant working to redesign operations have found higher levels of production with an alternative design.

The second option is for the leader to recruit a project manager. The project manager recruits team members, and as they come on board, they participate in interviewing and hiring.

Rather than assigning tasks individually, the teams review tasks together and assign those tasks based on individual skills and interests. The team meets weekly and reviews the work performed together and problem solves design and production issues together.

This organizational design is referred to as a cross-functional work group. The group has individual and team goals aligned with the organizational goals and is recognized and rewarded for improvements as a group. This design facilitates the cross-training of team members and stimulates the creativity and innovation required when leading multi-cultural and generational personnel for new product design and production.

An organization I recently served interviewed their clients, developed a new vision, mission, and strategy and identified performance measures for the organization.

They then reorganized around those strategic goals and measures so that each week they could measure their performance, problem solve, and get work done. The result was an organization that changed from producing 5–6 units per year to 12–14 units per year with higher levels of quality and customer satisfaction. The organization created new ideas faster, designed new services faster, and implemented those services in record time.

For this new organization to work effectively, the leader had to change. This leader had learned to tell his personnel what to do, how to do it, and when to do it. After coaching, he stopped offering solutions to problems completely, began asking staff for their ideas and when asked for a solution began asking staff how they would solve it.

He stopped managing individuals and managed the leaders of the work groups instead. He had been meeting monthly with staff members having key responsibilities and changed to meeting with his group leaders instead. Each week, this leadership team evaluated their performance measures and how they were working together. These changes in leadership behavior along with the new organizational structure led to growing levels of creative and innovative behavior throughout the organization.

Another client organized around their strategy and scorecard. The Financial Management group consisted of operations personnel along with human resources and accounting personnel. The Operations Performance group consisted of operations, engineering, real estate, accounting, and human resource personnel. Customer Satisfaction group consisted of operations, marketing, sales, real estate, and accounting personnel. Employee Satisfaction group had personnel from operations, human resources, and accounting. These groups met monthly to review goals and develop action plans for the coming month.

The benefit to engaging every part of the organization, involving them in information sharing, collaboration, and decision making generated better and more creative decisions for the organization. Efficiency and performance were significantly enhanced. This region improved from being last of all U.S. regions in Customer Satisfaction and Employee Satisfaction to first in both categories. Market share for the region soared.

Research from this client's corporate office revealed that it was not possible to increase customer satisfaction scores without simultaneously increasing employee satisfaction. Similar research was cited in the *Harvard Business Review*.

To increase employee satisfaction, each leader in the organization had to change from being a cop who told employees what to do, when to do it, and how to do it to being a coach who developed goals with staff, listened to them, and asked for ideas when problem solving and innovating. As these managers' behaviors changed, the organization became highly creative, innovative, and competitive in its market.

Linking Strategy, Staff, and Customers

I was asked to help a client set up high-performing work groups in her operation. She was aware that having her organization working in teams, knowing customer requirements and empowered to make work decisions was the basis of creativity and innovation throughout her operation. When touring her facility, I talked with several employees. Each one could tell me the client company they were producing for, who the contact people were in those companies and what and when they needed those products. This leader had been highly successful in linking her employees with the company's client base and building the business. She realized innovation occurs when your staff understands what exceeds customer expectations and continually works to do better.

Another client was a Quick Service Restaurant (QSR) corporation. They were committed to improving operational performance and customer satisfaction. In the process of designing collaborative work groups

Product/Service	Ratings 1 = Poor 5 = Excellent
Product quality	1 2 3 4 5
Service	1 2 3 4 5
Courtesy	1 2 3 4 5
Responsiveness	1 2 3 4 5
Overall satisfaction	1 2 3 4 5

Figure 3.1 Daily/weekly survey

in each unit, the corporate offices implemented balanced scorecards in each of its restaurants. Additionally, each shift in each restaurant had a balanced scorecard. Each restaurant developed a customer survey tool for daily use. The data were accumulated and plotted weekly on each shift's scorecard. This process linked staff with both customers and the corporate strategy creating clear focus and alignment (Figure 3.1).

The key to making the process work involved restaurant management. They reviewed scorecards with each shift team each week and changed their leadership behavior from controlling outcomes to collaborating with their employees on creative solutions for increasing customer satisfaction scores, improving operational performance, reducing food and labor costs, and increasing employee satisfaction. The operation reduced employee turnover by 60 percent while reducing labor costs and improving production accuracy.

During my work with this organization, a profit center leader was asked by a restaurant manager to visit her restaurant. As his coach, I was asked to come with him. When he entered the restaurant, things seemed different. The employees had talked with their customers and based on customer feedback had taken it upon themselves to redecorate the restaurant with flower baskets and a new coat of paint. They and the manager were smiling with pride when he entered. My client could not believe they would make such changes without talking with him first. In the past, he would have scowled and taken the manager to her office for a good talking to. However, this time he did not scowl, and instead smiled and congratulated them on their initiative. When he asked about restaurant performance, managers and crew were excited to report sales and customer satisfaction scores had increased since the changes. This restaurant manager had successfully linked her staff with their strategy and customers resulting in greater innovation within the restaurant and greater sales and market share for the company.

Alignment Survey

This survey is designed to help you and your staff discuss how well they are aligned with your organization's strategy and agree on what might be done to become better informed and aligned.

Rate the items mentioned in Figure 3.2 based on how you think your staff would rate them, then, ask your staff to complete the survey and compare results.

Behavior	No 1	Poor 2	Adequate 3	Good 4	Very Good 5
Have a balanced strategy based on the four pillars.					
Customers, suppliers, and employees participated in developing the strategy.					
Balanced scorecard is posted including graphs measuring progress on goals of the four pillars.					
Staff is organized around strategy and goals.					
Staff has input in decisions regarding organizational changes and their work.					
Strategy and staff are linked with customers.					
Customer satisfaction is continually measured.					
Staff determined goals for their areas of responsibility.					

Figure 3.2 Alignment survey

Stop	Start	Continue

Figure 3.3 Action plan

Plan of Action

Use Figure 3.3 to identify what to change to align your workforce with strategy and clients. First list behaviors your leader and workgroup identify as getting in the way of full alignment under STOP. Then list behaviors and actions leader and group members should begin under START. Finally, identify actions helping you and your staff and list those under CONTINUE.

$$\text{COMMUNICATE}$$

"In business know how to be a good leader and always try to bring out the best in people. It's very simple: listen to them, trusts in them, believe in them, respect them and let them have a go!"

—Sir Richard Branson

"Leaders foster partnership by making sure their mouths match their moves."

—Chip R. Bell, Managers as Mentors

CHAPTER 4

Getting It!

According to one of my Facebook friends, the greatest problem in communication is that we listen to reply rather than to understand. What is communication and what does it take to ensure flow of information between staff and their leader?

Communication is a process involving a sender, a message, and a receiver. The receiver, upon receiving the message, confirms receipt of the message creating a feedback loop (Figure 4.1).

The most important element of feedback involves identifying feelings.

Facts + Feelings = Full Message. You can usually determine the feelings of your receiver by viewing body language, in particular, facial expressions. If you as the receiver do not identify both facts and feelings when conveying the complete message back to sender, the chance of effective communication is diminished. The illustration points out the key reason for communication failure—lack of a feedback loop.

Technology hinders and helps organizations' communication. For example, e-mail is fast and efficient but creates challenges in which neither the sender nor receiver is able to easily understand the other's feelings. Or,

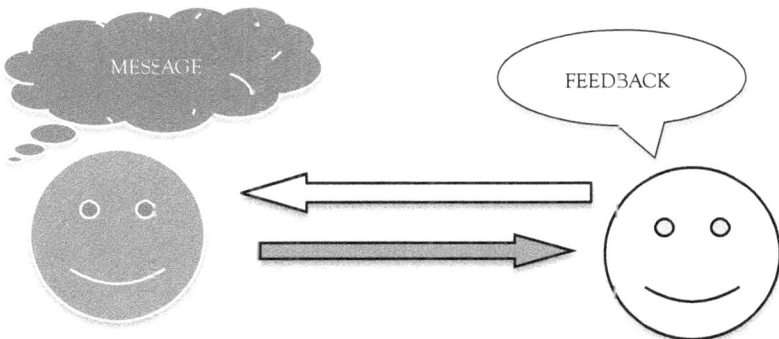

Figure 4.1 Feedback Loop

the receiver is occupied with other matters and does not read your message. (lol). To illustrate the importance we place on understanding feelings, we create symbols to communicate how we feel when using technology. ☐

Creating a continuous flow of information requires the leadership behaviors of Getting It, Meeting Regularly with Staff, Building Trust, and Modeling Ethical Behavior.

Many leaders feel that if they are not speaking with authority they will not be respected for their authority. A client I once coached described his first manager "driving him crazy" because of always answering his questions with a question. Only now that he has become a supervisor, did my client understand the value of helping others think through issues for themselves. It was a relief to know he was not responsible for having all the answers, he explained.

When assisting an airline maintenance organization changes their culture, I received a call one day to meet with the executive who had retained our services. He wanted to tell me about his experience several days earlier. When walking through the terminal to work one morning, he spotted an old friend walking alone and spoke to him. "Hello John, you don't seem to be feeling well today. What is wrong" he said. John started telling him about problems at home and did not stop talking until they reached an intersection, each going separate ways. My client explained that 3 days later, John came to his office to say how much he appreciated the interest shown on him. My client assured me that he said nothing, just listened to John all the way to work. Such is the power of listening.

If a leader fails to listen to associates, he or she will not succeed as a true leader. For that reason, it is critical to understand the elements of being a top-notch receiver of information.

To be a great listener, it is important to first clear your head and resolve to repeat what you have been told including any feelings expressed by the person in their message. Remember facts and feelings create a full message.

Open Questions

Many of our managers have learned to instruct and lead people to agree with their ideas. As a result, they fail to appreciate the power of listening and using to their best advantage open ended questions. Managers have told me they will lose control if they ask such questions. These managers already know what they want and use closed question to get support for those ideas. For example, "Wouldn't you agree we would be better off using Mohamed instead of Josh?"

Most leaders would agree we gain more control by using open questions rather than closed. These questions begin with What, Who, How, Why, Where, and When and require more than a yes or no answer. The purpose is to let your associates know you are open to hearing from them. By doing so, we gather much more information than with closed questions. Questions would sound something like this:

"Who do you think we should use?"
"When should they start?"
"How should they be oriented?"
"What should their first tasks be?"
Avoid questions as follows:
"I think we should use Mohamed and he can start Monday".
"You can get him oriented and I will have a list of assignments prepared".
"Don't you agree?"

Using these six words (What, Who, Why, How, Where, and When) to open your questions will immediately increase creativity in your organization. Take a minute and practice making open questions out of the questions below:

"I think we should go for pizza. Ok?"
"Wouldn't you agree we have enough staff for this project?"
"I think Dawn has the best idea, what about you?"

A supervisor told that after learning about open questions, he conducted a crew meeting with his construction crew. He simply asked, "What do you need to help you do your jobs better?" They all responded "New boots!" Many had shoes that were leaking and made their work uncomfortable. He got them boots. The next week he did the same thing. They said, "keep all the tools in one truck." He gave them permission to take care of it themselves. The next week, a crew member approached him and said, "We know you won't be here tomorrow but don't worry. We will take care of everything." Not only did they take care of everything, but crew performance improved.

Emotional Quotient

Expressing understanding of feelings is critical for driving out fear and providing encouragement. Here are four feelings to be aware of when listening for understanding and communicating a full message.

Joy has a range of emotions from feeling fine to feeling hysterical.
Fear has a range of feelings from some anxiety to frightened.
Anger has a range of feelings from slightly miffed to outrage.
Sorrow has a range of emotions from sad to depressed.

As discussed earlier, your ability to identify the feelings that accompany the facts of a message not only increases understanding, but also encourages additional information sharing. "You seem excited about joining us and working on the customer survey part of the project," or, "It sounds like you are pretty upset over the change in assignments."

We are tempted to advise our associates to not feel upset because everything will be better. That is not what they need to hear. They just need to know you get it. I heard a manager once say to a very frustrated employee, "No need to be getting upset, it won't help any." The employee's facial expression said clearly that his manager was not being helpful.

For years, when working out of town I would return home Thursday nights. I would ask my wife how things had gone. She would describe in detail the problems she had encountered during the week. Naturally, being a consultant, I would suggest solutions. She would get very angry with me (in the range of outrage). I finally realized a different approach was needed. The following week upon arriving home, I simply listened to her, did not say a word, and when she was through talking I said, "It sounds like you have had a tough week. You must be exhausted. Why don't we get a baby sitter and go out for dinner tomorrow night." Home life got much better. I had begun hearing her feelings and communicating what I was hearing.

It was hard for me as a husband to use the techniques I taught and coached managers to use. I can understand how difficult it may be for others to change and become true leaders through becoming great listeners.

Rephrase

Rephrasing is used to confirm what you are hearing and has proven helpful to many managers when needing to remember a prior discussion. It is also used to encourage someone to continue talking and is helpful when brainstorming or otherwise encouraging creativity in your workplace. It is used to confirm agreements and is also used to redirect conversation when it drifts off topic.

Rephrasing is simply repeating in your own words what the sender of the message is communicating to you. It is the basic tool used to close the communication feedback loop. Keep in mind that if the message is important, both the facts and feelings should be communicated back to the person talking with you. Several examples of this skill have already been discussed, but here is one more to help with understanding.

Your team member has come to you to explain that the application project has run off its tracks and is not only behind schedule but will experience major cost overruns. Not a good day for you or him. The conversation might go something like this, "Are you out of your ever lovin' mind?" However, you have been to our charm school and know that closed questions are out of the question. You are going to practice open questions and rephrasing that includes feeling statements. So, instead of a good chewing out, you say, "You sound concerned, what were the causes and how do you think we can get the project back on track?" Then, you might ask, "How can I help?"

Silence

Interestingly, enough silent and listen possess the same letters. Silence can be misunderstood and misused. Suffice it to say what it means is you do not interrupt and do not think of rebuttals or solutions while your employee, peer, or superior are talking. Just remain very quiet, clear your head and listen. A method for clearing your mind is to be prepared to tell them what they told you. By doing so and being completely quiet, you will ascertain the full message being conveyed. Your sender may already have determined the best course of action. So, close your lips and listen!

I was serving a 3M plant and had provided leadership training for their managers and supervisors. One day, a supervisor I was coaching called me to his office. He told me his manager had called in the union president to discuss growing conflicts in the department and had invited him to attend. He said the meeting lasted for more than 2 hours and the manager used all the listening skills you are learning in this chapter. During the meeting, the supervisor attempted to talk and his manager kicked him under the table to remain silent. At the end of the meeting, they learned the personnel issues all had to do with the fact the president did not receive positive feedback for his work and was bothered that neither he nor other crew members were being recognized for their efforts.

CHAPTER 5

Team Template

Meet Regularly with Staff

Creating a team structure is the foundation for communication with a steady flow of information and creating a collaborative and innovative operation. The leader must be able to lead the meetings in addition to conducting group and individual conversations. This requires the leader to become a facilitator using the listening skills described earlier as part of his or her skill set.

This is the story of a software company with offices in Atlanta, Georgia, and Seattle, Washington. An IT specialist in Atlanta had discussions on a broad array of projects over 6 years with his counterpart in Seattle. One day, the specialist in Atlanta asked his counterpart where in Seattle he lived. His counterpart said that he did not live in Seattle but lived in Atlanta. The specialist asked where his office was in Atlanta and was given an address on Peachtree Street. The specialist commented that he worked in the same building. When asked about location in the building, the counterpart said, "fourth floor". The specialist with surprise explained he worked on the same floor. He then asked where on the floor the counterpart worked, and when told, got up from his desk and turned to the person in the next office. It was his counterpart!

A team structure consisting of a weekly leadership team meeting and leaders then meeting with their teams throughout the organization within 24–48 hours enhances communication organization wide and speeds up response time as well. Imagine the two people in this story having a leader who believed in teamwork and collaboration. These two professionals would have been together in frequent communication meetings and would have solved problems and developed new products and services faster and with higher quality.

The elements of a meeting structure consist of regularly scheduled meetings and having great meetings. Meetings can be scheduled weekly, biweekly, or monthly and should be on the same day of week, time of day, and same location. The amount of time allocated to meetings is based on meeting frequency. One hour should be allocated for weekly meetings, biweekly meetings, 2 hours, and 4 hours for monthly meetings.

The reason for longer times for less frequent meetings is simply a matter of needing more time to cover additional topics that accrue over time. A client held 2-hour management meetings once per month. Each month they would complain about their meetings running over. Their actual meeting times were nearly 4 hours. Finally, with a little coaching, they agreed more time was necessary and allocated 4 hours for their monthly meetings.

Several factors contribute to great meetings. An agenda, published 2 days before the meeting, a code of conduct guiding meeting behavior, a time keeper for keeping discussions focused and a record keeper for minutes facilitate smoother running meetings. In meetings, work groups review their balanced scorecards (aligned with operation's strategy), collaborate to solve problems, make decisions together, innovate improvements with existing products and services, and create new products and services together.

The partners of a design and build company asked for training on conducting effective meetings. Upon training the partners and project managers, I had an opportunity to see them in action. One partner would offer an idea to the other partner who responded in turn to the other partner. It could have been a ping pong match. LOL. The project managers just sat there watching the partners talk to each other until the meeting concluded (Figure 5.1). After providing some just-in-time coaching, the partners began offering ideas and asking project managers for their ideas and solutions. A very difficult change for the partners but the change meant improvements in their small business.

Great Meeting Agenda

MEETING LEADER_____

TIME KEEPER_____

RECORD KEEPER_____

GATE KEEPER_____

Time	Topic	Person	Decision
9:00–9:02	Review Agenda	Suzanne	Approval of agenda
9:02–9:07	Member Recognition	Suzanne and all	
9:07–9:15	Review of Action Plan	Suzanne	Updated action plan
9:15–9:35	Problem Solving	Jeff	Solution for solvent breakdown
9:35–9:50	New Product Development Brainstorming	Betty Lou	Rough draft
9:50–9:55	Action Plan Update	Suzanne	Updated action plan
9:55–10:00	Meeting Assessment	Suzanne	Changes to meeting

Figure 5.1 Agenda example

Meeting Leader facilitates meeting discussions and decision making.

Time Keeper informs leader and team when time is up on a topic.

Leader asks group if they need more time.

Record Keeper updates and publishes the Action Plan.

Gate Keeper keeps members from changing topics and getting the meeting off track.

Code of Conduct

Great meetings that start and end on time and generate creative outcomes do not happen by themselves. One tool for creating productive meeting behaviors is the Code of Conduct. It also serves as a guide to ethical behavior. The Code of Conduct is a list of behaviors developed by the work group and is used to manage their meeting behavior and decisions. It is helpful to post the list on the wall in the meeting room for everyone to see during their meetings. Benefits to having a code of conduct include creating common expectations and understanding among group members, encouraging desirable behavior among members, enhancing the creativity of the group, and having a record of the guidelines. An example of a code of conduct is listed below and may be helpful as an example when leading a group through deciding on a list of meeting behaviors for themselves.

Code of Conduct Example

1. Start and End on Time
2. Discussions Stay in the Room
3. No Side Conversations
4. Turn off Electronic Devices during Meeting
5. Be Positive
6. Stay on Topic
7. Do What We Say We Will Do
8. Encourage Creativity
9. Be Frank and Honest

Typically, the Gatekeeper monitors the code during meetings. If people are having a side conversation, the Gatekeeper simply calls out the number, in this case, "number 3!" A client was using an industrial psychology group to help with an issue. We were having lunch one day and I was describing how the process worked. "So you are the one!", they exclaimed. "We were in a meeting yesterday with a union group and everyone was yelling numbers at each other!" The group was self-monitoring and having a great meeting, they reported.

Action Plan

The action plan is the glue to making innovation happen and ideas being taken to design and implementation. It is a form of accountability that is used to recognize achievements and problem solve roadblocks to accomplishing goals. Many meetings I have attended end in frustration because

What	Who	When	Status
Develop product enhancement specifications	Andrew	3/15	
First draft of new application design	Gilly	6/15	
Contact 3 clients regarding new application design	Daniel Hannah Hank	4/15	

Figure 5.2 Action plan example

as the meeting participants say, "Nothing ever gets done, we are just spinning our wheels." The action plan fixes such problems and an example is illustrated in Figure 5.2.

The updated action plan is distributed at end of meeting by the record keeper and is included with agenda when published two days before next meeting.

Meeting Evaluation

Evaluate the meetings you are now attending. Identify what you like about them and what you would change. List your ideas and thoughts using Figure 5.3.

What I Like	What We Should Change

Figure 5.3 Meeting evaluation

CHAPTER 6

Effectively Expressing Messages

Thus far we have discussed the critical skills of listening for understanding, i.e., getting it, and the importance of the leader being a great listener with staff members and during group meetings. The second part of the communication process involves effectively communicating messages to individuals and groups. The key to communicating messages that are easily received is to make them concise and to the point. Tailoring the message to your audience is also helpful. For example, here are some examples to help you communicate concisely with millennials in text or e-mail:

BRB = Be Right Back
LOL = Lots of Laughs
TTYL = Talk To You Later
SYS = See You Soon
SMH = Shaking My Head
WRUD = What are You Doing
LMAO = Laughing My Ass Off
WTF = What the F***
GR8 = Great
IDK = I Don't Know
AF = As F***ed
JK = Just Kidding
IDC = I Don't Care
YOLO = You Only Live Once

There are three work situations in which a leader has the need for critical communication with staff members. The first situation involves performance of concern issues, the second situation concerns the need to resolve conflicts and reach agreement between individuals or groups, and the third situation concerns the need to persuade rather than dictate to staff.

Correct Concerning Behavior

Most performance problems are due to a lack of human resource systems or ineffective use of such systems. The person may lack adequate feedback on poor performance or never receive recognition for desired performance. When a performance problem occurs, it is important to approach the person as if he or she wants to perform well. If you assume the person is just unmotivated, there will be the tendency to blame the person and escalate the situation thus making it worse. To set the stage for providing feedback, have a location that is private. Be sure to listen first in order to understand the person's point of view and their reasons for the undesirable behavior. After hearing their point of view, use the process shown in Figure 6.1 for helpful correcting the behavior of concern:

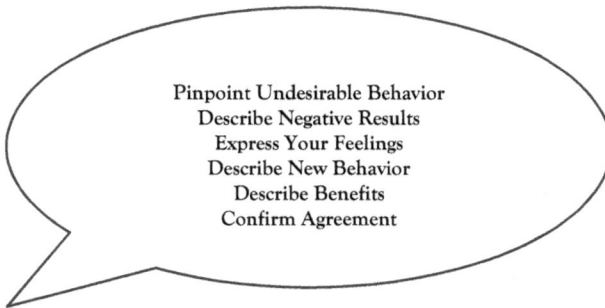

Pinpoint Undesirable Behavior
Describe Negative Results
Express Your Feelings
Describe New Behavior
Describe Benefits
Confirm Agreement

Figure 6.1 Steps for correcting

1. Pinpoint the Undesirable Behavior

Describe the behavior of concern specifically enough that the behavior can be counted and measured. Do not describe character traits such as "you seem lazy" or "You seem like you just don't care." There is nothing they can do to change your perceptions and will argue with you. However, if you describe the specific behavior, "You are arriving late to work nearly every day and never call to let us know" they know exactly what you are concerned with and can begin having a constructive conversation.

2. Describe the Negative Results of Their Behavior

Many times your personnel may not know how their behavior is affecting you or your business. Letting them know the impact of their behavior can be helpful to them. For example, "When you come to work late and don't call to let us know, more work is created for everyone else and I do not know if I should call in someone to replace you."

3. Express Your Feelings

People typically care about other's feelings. Letting this person know how it affects you and how you feel can increase understanding of how their behavior is affecting others and their manager. If you believe they do not care how you feel, skip this step. For example, "When you are late and do not call it not only creates more work for everyone but also makes me very anxious because I am unsure about what steps I should take."

4. Describe the Behavior You Desire

Specifying an alternative behavior makes this model helpful in that the person with the behavior of concern now knows what to do differently. In most cases, it is helpful to solicit the person's ideas, as they may know of other solutions that would work for them. For example: "When you are going to be late for work and do not call it makes more work for us all. Therefore, I want you to come to work on time. How do you plan to make that happen?"

5. Describe the Benefits of the New Behavior

Letting this person know how their new behavior can benefit your operation helps you "sell" the idea. However, describing how the new behavior will benefit the person helps them buy into changing their behavior. For example, "When you come to work on time you will increase your weekly take home pay and improve relationships with everyone here."

6. Confirm Agreement

Before concluding the discussion, seek commitment by asking, "What do you think?" Using an open- ended question you will learn how they feel and increase the likelihood of success.

Convert Conflict to Cooperation

Most of the time conflicts or disagreements occur because of misunderstandings, lack of resources, or challenging work processes. There is a tendency to avoid discussing the issues as no one wants to create conflict and conversations may become unpleasant. This tends to create more conflict and greater tension within the workplace. A process exists that offers people in conflict a chance to be heard and an opportunity to resolve their conflict. The process includes the following steps (Figure 6.2):

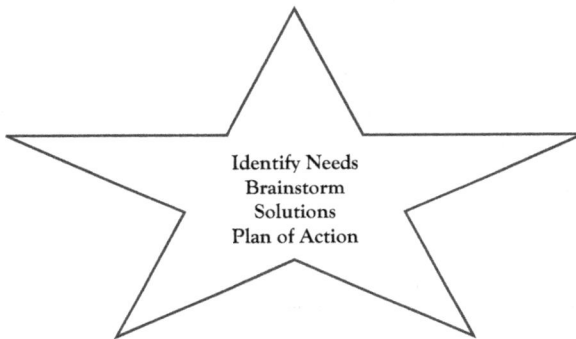

Figure 6.2 Conflict to cooperation process

1. ***Identify the Needs of Each Person in the Conflict***

   Participants will begin talking about what they want rather than what they need. For example, a person may want a salary increase but in talking about the raise will describe a need to be recognized for their good works. Two employees wanted the other to leave the office. The facilitator asks each person to describe their needs and encourages the other people in the conflict to listen and be prepared to rephrase the person's comments. Needs identified after much discussion included person #1 feeling insulted by the other's way of talking and Person #2 did not like #1 talking about her behind her back.

2. ***Brainstorm Solutions to Address Needs***

   The facilitator leads a brainstorming exercise in which each person has the opportunity to create solutions to resolve needs. After the brainstorming is completed participants, select the critical few

(20 percent) that resolve the needs listed earlier. The facilitator continues the discussion, maintaining respect among all participants, until agreement has been reached between the people in conflict. For example, Person #1 offered solutions to address needs for different choices of words and talking behind #2's back. Then, #2 does the same. After the two have exhausted all options, the facilitator then asked them to select the solutions that address the needs of both.

3. *Develop a Plan of Action*

The WHAT (solutions), WHO (persons implementing the solutions), and the WHEN (each solution will be implemented) are written down and given to each person. The final step is agreeing on a time to meet again and review results of the agreement.

Friendly Persuasion

When developing a creative and innovative environment, the leader may use persuasion to encourage staff members to risk offering "out of the box" ideas or to participate on a design team. Additionally, many organizations are using contractors (1099's) to avoid the additional cost of hiring full time employees. These contractors have the ability to go wherever they wish to work and expect to be treated with respect. It becomes a critical skill for leaders who coordinate and manage contractors and volunteers. The persuasion process includes the following steps (Figure 6.3):

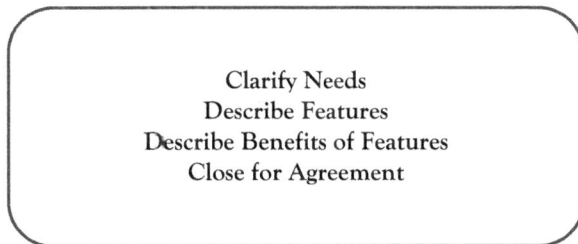

Clarify Needs
Describe Features
Describe Benefits of Features
Close for Agreement

Figure 6.3 Persuasion process

1. *Clarify Needs of the Person*

   This involves creating an understanding of the personal or professional goals of the individual involved. For example, "Jean I know you are interested in moving into marketing as part of your professional growth with our firm." "Is that correct?"

2. *Describe Features*

   Features are the key components of your proposal, product or service. For example, "Well Jean, the upcoming design team assignment might help. You will be meeting with professionals and management throughout the company, the team will be researching our market for new ideas, and new product ideas will transform into new products."

3. *Describe Benefits*

   Benefits are the WIIFM or What Is In It For Me discussion. For example, "Being on this team may take more time at work but you will be connected with people who can help you move into marketing, you will have full knowledge of the new products coming on line and will have developed the capability to represent our firm and new products to existing and new markets. You will have become fully trained on key parts of marketing activities through participation on this design team."

4. *Close for Agreement*

   When discussing the person's readiness to accept your proposal, it is beneficial for the leader to first ask how they feel about the proposal. It is important to listen closely for their concerns and needs. You can then address those concerns and close by offering the person a choice. For example, "Well it sounds as if we reassign the administrative part of the project, this could work for you." "Would you want to begin this month or the beginning of next month?"

In this new normal economy with market and technology changes buffeting all organizations, it becomes incumbent for business owners and managers to apply these tools in order to create a culture of respect and innovation in a diverse workplace.

CHAPTER 7

Encourage Ethical Efforts

Ethics is defined as conforming to principles of right versus wrong. Ethics has also been defined as taking into account how your behavior affects others and how corporate behavior affects the community. It is the manner in which one individual treats another and the manner in which an enterprise (public and private) treats both its employees and its community. Recently, I heard morality defined as how we treat people we know and ethics defined as how we treat people we do not know.

I have heard it said our nation seems focused on "me first" and gaining as much wealth as possible. This sentiment sees our nation being based on competition with no consequences for cheaters, Wall Street bankers being frequently mentioned to make the point. As a nation, we are seen to lack the will or mechanisms needed to control unethical behavior within both the private and public sectors of our economy.

In order to change this culture, organizations and communities must install controls rewarding ethical behavior and punishing cheating behavior of individuals, business owners, and public service officials. To illustrate, recently the criminal conviction of a peanut butter company's CEO made national news. The conviction was so rare it was seen as newsworthy by national news organizations.

Ben Bernanke, former Chairman of the Federal Reserve stated in a USA Today interview regarding the recent financial crisis, "More corporate executives should have gone to jail. The Justice Department and other law enforcement agencies focused on indicting financial firms. He notes, it would have been my preference to have more investigation of individual action, since obviously everything that went wrong or was illegal was done by some individual, not by an abstract firm."

It has been said that the first step leading to unethical behavior is when someone says, "no one will notice." Encouraging associates to speak up when ethical challenges are seen is discouraged by the manner in which organizations treat Whistleblowers. Blaming the messenger occurs often and provides employees with little support or encouragement for challenging unethical behavior. Consider how many employees of Volkswagen knew about the intentional violation of emission control regulations. Why did no one in Germany or in the United States blow the whistle on these cheating behaviors? The culture either encourages ethical behavior or unethical lapses in behavior. Volkswagen's top down, central command structure was described as creating a culture rewarding obedience and discouraging freedom of expression.

The economic crisis created by Wall Street misdeeds and weak regulation has created the need for business leaders to earn public trust once again. Public polls rate large corporations at nearly the same low level as congress. How ethical is it for the auto companies to calculate the cost of deaths versus the cost of a recall, how ethical is it for our universities to use PhD's for associate professorships in order to reduce labor costs while at the same time presidents and chancellors are receiving larger and larger salaries and bonuses. Not to mention coaches and the ethical lapses regarding student athletes and the quality of their education. Such behavior is encouraging professors and student athletes to form unions. Recently, I was told about a healthcare organization with few employees over the age of 35. The organization's practice is to keep staff until they reach a certain salary threshold, terminate them, and hire younger personnel who will earn less.

How ethical is it for our states to put the burden of education costs on students rather than designating adequate funding for public education? How ethical is it for hospitals to tell indigent patients care will be free only to hire attorneys and collection agencies to aggressively collect fees from these same patients when released from care? What is the ethical rationale for an oil company or power company refusing to remediate the pollution they caused?

Our economic system continues to experience the struggle between a commitment to principles and the pursuit of wealth. This struggle permeates every facet of our economy from financial institutions, to healthcare, energy, education, technology, and manufacturing. These organizations range from small to mid-size and multinational corporations and nonprofits. This struggle has been described as the tension between free markets and the public good. We hear the tension when a business owner says, "I take pride in making the finest beer using the best grains available and pay more if needed" or "If you have to decide whether to document your activities for billing purposes or help a client, you had better be serving your client!" to comments like, "Regulations are strangling our free-market system" and "let the markets decide." These sentiments are neither right nor wrong. They are however, out of balance and tend to drive a business out of business.

How do leaders maintain ethical standards in times of challenge to financial well-being? As long as leaders maintain top of mind awareness regarding their principles, publicly post those principles, publicly recognize employees who speak up when witnessing violations and punish violators, a culture of ethical behavior can be created. Maintaining an ethical compass leads to creating a culture of innovation and a sustainable organization.

A client held weekly meetings with staff. They reviewed rumors in the department at each meeting. If a rumor was false the message was communicated to all employees. If a rumor was partially true or true, the management team confirmed the rumor with its employees. It was critically important that everyone knew the truth. This was a matter of ethical behavior to this management team. Several IT firms informed their customers when asked to provide personal information to the government. Ethical behavior was critical to these leaders' business strategy.

This tension between conforming to principles and pursuing wealth provides drivers for helping us understand leader integrity and ethical challenges. Figure 7.1 is an illustration of the performance levels of organizations and is a Moral Compass designed to help organizations examine their current situation and take steps where necessary.

I know of no organization functioning with a lack of principles to guide them and lack of drive to pursue wealth. However, there are nonprofits who have clearly defined principles and tend to pursue those principles without regard for capital accumulation. In every case, they struggle to be sustainable. We can all think of companies who overlooked their principles in the pursuit of wealth such as Enron, Lehman Brothers, AIG, Arthur Anderson, and Standard and Poor, to name a few. It is true that we can live for a time by simply ignoring what is right and blindly pursuing wealth. The data say however this journey is short lived. A much more sustainable way to operate a business is through a balanced approach of pursuing wealth through the lens of your organization's principles (Figure 7.2).

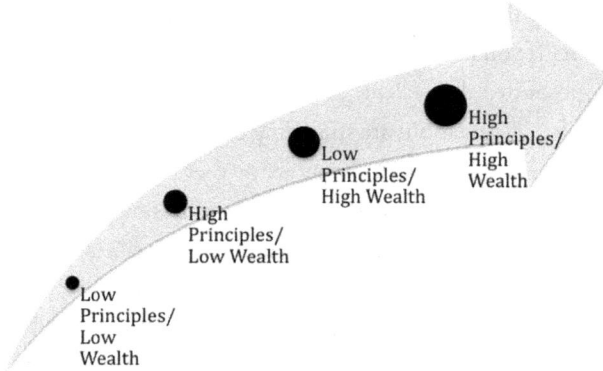

Figure 7.1 Ethics and success model

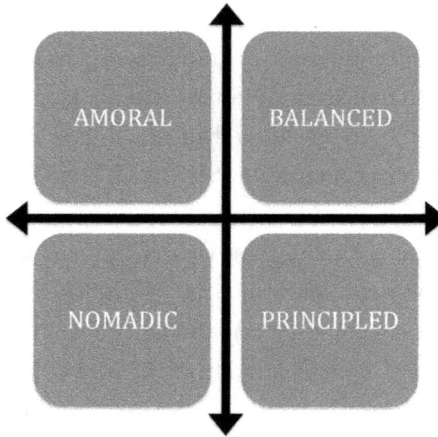

Figure 7.2 Ethical compass

Ethical Compass

Amoral

Low principles, high wealth

This organization focuses on wealth creation and conveys the message that the end justifies the means. As an example, a national financial services institution mandated goals for each unit to generate specified amounts in fees from each customer. This same institution was recently fined for the practice and was earlier convicted of red-lining certain neighborhoods from either qualifying for loans or being charged higher rates for the same loans provided to other neighborhoods.

Nomadic

Low Principles, Low Wealth

This organization drifts and can be identified by the mix of products and services that lack connection with one another. Leadership lacks focus and is unpredictable in expectations of associates and direction of the organization. A nonprofit was successful creating and passing legislation for cleaner air. Afterward it drifted and began participating in other endeavors having less and less relevance to clean air initiatives.

Principled

High Principles, Low Wealth

This organization has a reputation for doing good works and its leader is respected within the organization and community. However, the devotion to principles pulls the leader from attending to the financial well-being of the organization. There is continual stress between doing good and making ends meet. A number of non-profits failed during the recession as a result.

Balanced

High Principles, High Wealth

This organization takes a balanced approach to its business. Clearly stated principles are evident and staff can describe how each principle is practiced. Everyone knows the organization's financial status and works to enhance its financial well-being. These organizations are described as being highly transparent.

With which of these quadrants would your organization align? Consider your current emphasis on principles. Then consider your focus on creating wealth by increasing revenues and reducing costs (Figure 7.3).

An inventory is provided as follows. Our workshops facilitate scoring the inventory for positioning on the Ethical Compass.

1. We are encouraged to be frank and honest.
2. We do whatever it takes to exceed customer expectations.
3. We are rewarded for revealing misdeeds.
4. We receive monthly financial updates.
5. We have a written set of principles posted for everyone to see.
6. We base our decisions on costs.
7. We adhere to our principles when pursing our goals.
8. We avoid charging hidden or add-on fees.
9. Our employees are paid fairly and earn at least a living wage.
10. We are encouraged to take initiative with clients.
11. We tell customers when they do not need a product or service we offer.
12. We are rewarded and receive credit for identifying problems and implementing solutions at work.
13. Our leaders tell us the truth and show respect.
14. We make fact-based decisions.
15. Employees tell each other the truth and show respect.
16. Employees are provided the tools, resources, and training to perform their duties.
17. We value the air, water, and land around us and strive to protect it.
18. We invest the money required to protect our environment from pollution

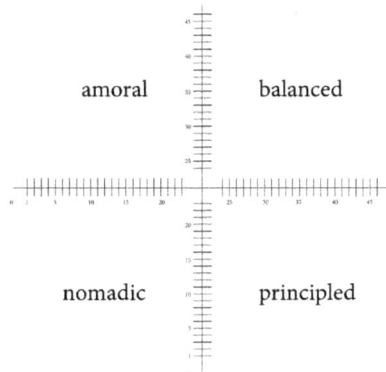

Figure 7.3 Ethics evaluation tool

Create Trust

There are many ways to erode trust and discourage creativity and innovation. A colleague of mine who works in mental health gave an example. He told the story of offering an idea to help with a difficult case in a staff meeting. The program director commented on how silly the idea was, sent an e-mail commenting on how bad the idea was and made humorous comments in the following staff meeting regarding the idea. My friend confided that he refrains from commenting in meetings now and will certainly not offer ideas again.

I have often told the story about my father going to work for a company having three unions. On a visit home Dad told me he had just set a company record for most grievances filed against a manager in 1 month. Things were a bit rocky he explained. Several weeks later, we were talking and he told me that after several sleepless nights he decided it was time to talk to his crew. So he called them together on a Monday morning and asked them why they were so hostile toward him. "You don't trust us" they said. They explained that he seemed to always be checking up on them and they did not like the message it was giving. Dad explained that he had a boss who frequently wanted to know the status of projects and he needed to be ready with answers. The union suggested that he check with them at the end of each day and Dad agreed. The grievances stopped. Dad had begun building trust with his crew.

Building trust is accomplished when there is an environment of open and free flowing communication. Creating such an environment includes the following leadership actions:

1. **Keeps staff current on organizational plans and activities.**
   Providing information on activities and decisions along with the rationale helps your staff make better decisions and feel more in the know and part of your organization.
2. **Provides needed information to staff.**
   Learn from your associates the kind of information they need and be certain they have regular and frequent updates on progress toward goal attainment and improvements. Let them know what information is important and you wish to receive from them.

3. **Is honest and direct with staff.**
   Provide clear information on both the good and bad news providing time for discussion and your honest assessment of the situation. Clarity and honesty will build trust over time.

4. **Doesn't shoot the messenger.**
   Reflective listening helps to prevent defensiveness when receiving bad news. Be sure to avoid attributing blame to the person providing the news and thank them for the message. A software development Director solicited a status update from his project manager. When she informed him the project was behind schedule and several problems had occurred during the project phase, she was terminated. No more bad news was shared within his department.

5. **Encourages free flow of information among staff members.**
   There is no need for the leader to control all information flow and he or she could not do it if they wanted to do so. By encouraging associates to have informal meetings to share information and discuss projects you are creating an open climate for communication and building trust.

6. **Encourages staff to challenge the status quo.**
   Thanking someone for challenging your position on an issue creates an environment for creativity. Listening, using rephrasing, and encouraging them to share their ideas and reasons sets the stage for you to respectfully share your reasoning for your idea with them. Such dialogue leads to an open and creative work environment.

7. **Responds quickly to staff communications and needs.**
   "He promises a lot but rarely delivers" is a comment I hear frequently when interviewing staff before coaching a client. "My word is my bond" is another. Your staff learns to trust you and count on you by the actions you take when they express needs for assistance. Be sure to let them know what you can do and when you can do it. Then be certain to follow up as promised. Personnel and peers learn quickly if they are able to count on you when you make commitments. I know you have had the experience of working with people who promise to help but fail to follow through or make excuses for not doing what was promised. This quickly erodes trust. Admitting errors and following through on commitments is critical to your success in building trust as a leader.

8. **Speaks calmly and with respect.**

An executive I coached had created much loyalty among his leadership team. However, he also could be highly intimidating when he got upset, using profanity with a loud voice to make his points and subdue his staff. When I commented on this behavior with him, he denied actually acting in such a way. To make the point, he explained he asked his staff if he actually shouted and used profanity. Everyone agreed that he never shouted and cursed! What a surprise. However, after receiving feedback, I learned that he had curtailed both raising his voice and cursing behaviors. This was an exceptional leader who processed feedback and changed his intimidating behavior.

TRUST=Keep staff current+Provide Needed Information+ Honest&Direct+No Shooting the Messenger+Encourage free flow information among staff+Encourage staff to challenge status quo+Respond quickly to staff needs+Speak calmly & respectfully.

Behavior	No 1	Poor 2	Adequate 3	Good 4	Very Good 5
Leader listens without interrupting.					
Leader asks our opinions.					
Leader offers quality feedback on our performance.					
Leader follows through on commitments.					
Leader speaks calmly and with respect.					
Leader meets with us weekly or biweekly.					
Leader provides needed information.					
We use an agenda, code of conduct, and action plan in our meetings.					
We have developed a clear set of principles that we follow.					
Leader is truthful and can be trusted.					

Figure 7.4 Communication survey

Communication Survey

Complete the survey in Figure 7.4 as you believe your staff would answer it. Then, ask your group to complete the survey and compare notes before creating a plan of action.

Plan of Action

After completing your survey, consider the lessons learned and list the items you believe your leader and workgroup should start doing in order to improve communication under START. Then list the behaviors creating barriers to good communication and list those under STOP. Finally, recognize the good things you are doing and list those under CONTINUE in order to ensure you maintain those behaviors in your new culture (Figure 7.5).

Start	Stop	Continue

Figure 7.5 Action plan

$$\text{COLLABORATE}$$

While in the past we may have wanted loyal employees, today we need flexible people who are not possessive about "the way things are done around here."

—Spencer Johnson, Who Moved My Cheese?

CHAPTER 8

Create an Open Climate

Unless you are able to channel Steve Jobs, creativity and innovation occur with collaboration. Collaboration relies on leadership behaviors of facilitating, driving out fear, encouraging new ideas, and delegating.

When should you collaborate with your staff? You should collaborate when improving existing work processes and products, when initiating development of new products or services and when decisions you are making impact the group. If you are considering new technology and they must use it, they should be part of the discussion and decision. If you are considering standard dress codes or hiring an additional staff member your staff will be affected and you will need their support. Be certain to include them in your considerations before acting on your decision.

When developing a new automobile engine, Ford empowered engineers and crew members to create a new engine and drive train. The design group included production members in order to ensure the engine could be produced using a new manufacturing process. The engine was developed in record time and went into production without the normal start up production problems. In order for associates to create and innovate, several behaviors are required of their leaders. Those behaviors include driving out fear, encouraging new ideas, facilitating groups, and delegating responsibilities.

Ferret Out Fear

When working for a software company as Director of Human Resources, managers would come to the office to talk. A clear description of our work environment was found in the parting salutation, "Keep your head down." These managers felt it only a matter of time before they would be blamed and terminated for a problem they had no control over.

The personnel in this software company were managed through intimidation. The president hired retired military Colonels and higher rank to run key developmental and support operations. The president's leadership team developed confidential policies to terminate anyone whose spouse worked for another software development company. A project manager was terminated when she told the truth about development progress. Our department was directed to not hire gay or lesbian personnel, and each month the president reviewed health claims of the five persons having the highest insurance claims. The corporate lawyer yelled at people if he did not get his way. The result was high turnover, low productivity, incomplete projects, or projects having errors that could have been avoided. Fear was driven out of this organization by replacing the CEO with a leader from IBM. Then, the new leader visited departments to learn needs and invited programmers rather than senior management to review project progress with clients. He initiated an employee satisfaction survey and within a year several vice president and director level managers left the company. The culture began to change and software projects were completed and released on time.

In addition to using a culture assessment and implementing needed changes, there are other techniques used to break the tension and anxiety within an organization. An IT manager wanted to create a new environment in his department. In one of his weekly staff meetings, he put a blank piece of legal paper at each person's place. When they were seated he asked them to write down everything they thought wrong in the department, offer ideas for improvement, and put their notes under the door of his office. He then left the meeting. The next week this manager presented his staff's comments on a flip chart. Their ideas were organized into three categories: "Things I Control," "Things Our VP Controls," and "Things Neither I nor our VP Control." Together they created a plan of action for resolving the issues under their control. Anxiety and conflicts were resolved.

I was asked to help eliminate fear and anxiety in a mental health program. There were several psychologists and a number of MSW professionals creating conflicts and high anxiety within the program. My task was to provide an intervention to assist the group begin working together.

I chose a process using posted notes. Posted notes are usually quite useful when dealing with tension in a group because everyone can answer honestly without divulging their identity. Many times just having staff write down the issues reduces group tension. Using a problem-solving model for the exercise, everyone was asked to list key issues in the program on post-it notes and hand them to me. The notes were placed randomly on the flip chart so no one would be identified with their notes.

After the group organized the notes into problem categories, they were asked to discuss the meaning of the messages on the board. Everyone began to relax.

The group was asked to list solutions on post-it notes for each category of issues and to place their notes under the appropriate problem category. When asked, they easily discussed their solutions and began developing an action plan for implementing those solutions. The leader chose to participate as a member of the group and acknowledged his role in creating the fear and anxiety by refusing to address issues. He committed to his group the changes he would make and promised their action plan would be reviewed in upcoming staff meetings until all solutions were implemented. This leader took a big step toward leading a more creative and supportive workplace. He showed his humanness and gained the trust of his staff in the process.

One of the greatest causes of fear in the workplace is blame. Looking for someone to blame for something gone wrong or your making a mistake. Blaming is the result of anger and provides the release of pressure inside you. Something happens such as running out of supplies. We look for the first person we can blame for the problem knowing we should have followed up ourselves. Someone is singled out for blame. Afterward no one feels better and the problem continues to exist. Our blaming others has not helped! We have discouraged any initiative that existed among those with whom we work.

An airline I served had one of the best safety records in the industry. I believe the reason for their success was attributable to their emphasis on eliminating fear within their workforce. If their mechanics were afraid to alert others of an error or potential error lives could be in danger. As a result, supervisors and foremen were thoughtful in their responses to feedback and congratulated any mechanic who identified missing paperwork, missing information on paperwork or other errors. There was no blame in this workplace.

You may have heard the story of an IBM executive who met with his superior to submit his resignation. When asked for a reason, he explained he had just calculated the results of the project he had been assigned and the numbers indicated a $2 million loss. His boss replied, "Now why would I want you to leave after having just invested $2 million in you?" This leader emphasized learning rather than blaming. He realized he could either create an atmosphere of avoidance for new project assignments or create a culture in which engineers welcome the challenge to create and innovate.

There are several solutions to help any manager drive out fear.

1. **First, take responsibility for mistakes in your workplace.**
   Coaches praise their teams when they win and take responsibility when they lose. How many times have you heard the term "my bad" when someone is taking responsibility for their actions or point to themselves when throwing a ball out of bounds? A manager once told me that when she began taking responsibility for things going wrong in her workplace, loyalty among staff increased and performance improved because associates were no longer afraid to risk offering ideas and making decisions.

2. **Approach problems as an opportunity to be creative.**
   By taking responsibility for our actions and the actions of our work group we are able to apply the second solution. It allows us to approach problems as opportunities. For example, if your department has run out of medical supplies, the alternative to finding someone to blame is to take responsibility and problem solve. First conduct a cause analysis by asking "why" five times (The Five Why's). Then ask for solutions to resolve the key causes. Problem solving drives out fear and builds commitment. You will receive honest feedback and communication that leads to collaboration with staff.

3. **Give yourself permission to be human.**
   I have often assured managers, especially new ones, that it is permissible to be human and make mistakes. No one expects managers to be perfect, only to continue learning from their experiences. Even

managers make mistakes. Admitting to an error of judgment, a bad decision or forgetfulness earns respect and builds working relationships. When I realized this truth, life as a manager and husband became easier and relationships with staff and family strengthened. The same can be true for you!

From Dictator to Facilitator

A climate of creativity is established when leaders refrain from being dictators and become facilitators to begin leading their associates to generate new ideas. Corporate executives visited a plant I had served for several months. They met with various departments and afterward commented on how professional the management team provided agendas for meetings and used flip charts to facilitate comments and encourage free flowing exchange of ideas and information.

A supervisor for an airline met with his maintenance crew. Using a flip chart, he asked the union brothers to determine a better process for performing critical aircraft preventative maintenance checks. He led them in brainstorming new ideas, offering none of his own. The result was a new maintenance procedure that reduced the inspection and correction process from over 135 days to 75 days or less and performed with higher quality! That is innovation at its best.

I have listened to leaders moan and groan that their people do not work together and do not take initiative on projects. It is not employees who need to learn new behaviors, instead, it is their leaders who need to learn how to facilitate and delegate in a multigenerational and multi-cultural workplace.

Facilitation requires utilization of the listening skills described earlier, only now in a group setting. Those skills include open questions to gather information, expressing empathy to provide encouragement, rephrasing ideas and agreements to ensure understanding and using silence to encourage further participation. There are three ways to facilitate group brainstorming and each requires the leader to refrain from engaging in the discussion.

To become a facilitator, the leader focuses on generating ideas from the group rather than offering ideas and helping the group make decisions rather than making decisions for them. If the leader believes she is not able to be impartial and objective, she can ask another member of the team to act as facilitator. I once worked with an organization whose managers had all been quite controlling. They met with staff to inform them of upcoming events and pass along information. Rarely did an employee speak during the meetings. One week I witnessed a major culture change. One of the more controlling managers was sitting with her associates. An hourly employee was standing at the flip chart taking notes and serving as the facilitator for the session. They were brainstorming ideas to improve the way work was performed in their department. Major changes were implemented within the same month.

In order to optimize group discussion, persons should be sitting around a table rather than sitting classroom style in order for members to effectively communicate with other participants. Additionally, everyone should be able to see their comments recorded on the board. This verifies they have been heard and stimulates additional ideas and creativity.

The leader asks the group for ideas and using a flip chart or smart board records the ideas without comment other than to repeat for understanding and to ask "What else" in order to stimulate additional ideas.

1. **Free Wheeling**

   The purpose of Free Wheeling is to stimulate a burst of energy and ideas.

   Free Wheeling is what it sounds like. The group is asked for ideas by the facilitator who then becomes silent. Persons randomly offer ideas and those ideas are recorded using the same words offered by the participants. Either the person facilitating the meeting or a record keeper can record ideas. When ideas cease, the facilitator asks the question differently. For example, first question might be, "How can we expand the use of our gizmo to other markets?" The follow-up question might be, "What would our largest 4 clients suggest for expanded application of this gizmo?" By asking the group to move away from their ideas and to look through the lens of others, new ideas emerge.

2. **Round Robin**

   The purpose of Round Robin is to ensure everyone has an opportunity to speak. The leader asks an open question and begins calling on people starting on either side. As an introduction, the facilitator should let the group know that everyone will be asked for ideas and can either pass or share ideas. As a facilitator, I have found that using Free Wheeling first, then shifting to Round Robin is a good way to generate creative ideas and insure everyone is provided the opportunity to speak. Often the quiet person who shares nothing in Free Wheeling provides the jewel of an idea when asked in Round Robin. This method is also good to use with groups who are more deliberative and like having time to organize their thoughts. (Engineers come to mind!) By calling on each person around the table the other group members have the advantage of hearing ideas and planning their idea before being called upon.

3. **Slip**

   The purpose of the Slip Method is for silent brainstorming. It is good for generating ideas when fear or anxiety exists within the group.

   Group collaborative software can be useful for silent work; however, group members will be reluctant to participate if there is even a hint the ideas will be tracked back to them. For that reason, the use of post-it notes for Slip Method with flip charts achieves a certain level of trust. A pack of post-it notes is given to each participant with sharpie pens. Each person writes as many ideas as possible, each idea on a separate note. After their data dump, they take their notes to the flip chart and post them. After everyone has posted their notes, the facilitator reviews each one asking for clarification when needed.

Brainstorming Guidelines

Unless the group has much experience, guidelines should be reviewed before beginning a brainstorming session.

1. **All ideas are good ideas.**

   The group will need encouragement to risk not being judged for their comments.

2. **No criticizing ideas.**

   Criticizing ideas discourages participation not only of the person feeling criticized but other group members as well.

3. **No discussing ideas while listing them.**

    If the group asks questions for clarification of an idea or begins talking about how it would work the brainstorming ends and the group gets bogged down. Be sure to keep the group on track listing as many ideas as possible to keep focused and avoid veering off task.

4. **Go for quantity.**

    Quality ideas are generated using brainstorming and the more ideas the more quality ideas. Just continue encouraging group members to share ideas.

5. **Build on other ideas.**

    One of the reasons for recording ideas on a flip chart is to confirm what the person is saying. The other reason is to stimulate greater creativity. As group members see their ideas, more ideas come to mind. That creates excitement and leads to creativity and innovation.

6. **Clarify understanding of items on flip chart after brainstorming.**

    The time for discussing ideas occurs after the group has run out of ideas. At that point, the facilitator asks the group for questions and comments regarding anything on the flip chart. Only after there are no more comments does the facilitator begin sorting out the key ideas.

7. **Use the 80/20 rule for sorting ideas.**

    The idea that a group must work on everything on the list is part of every group's assumptions. However, that becomes a total waste of time because selecting key ideas will cover many if not all the ideas needing to be addressed. The concept is that choosing 20 percent of the items will take care of 80 percent of the issues. Ask yourself how many people occupy most of your time? Answer is usually around 20 percent. How many customers take 80 percent or more of your time? After your count you may find that approximately 20 percent of your customer base is taking 80 percent or more of your time. So when brainstorming, select 20 percent of the items that will have the most impact on the issue being addressed.

8. **Avoid comments such as "That won't work here" or "We tried that before and it didn't work."**

    Every organization has people who have been discouraged when showing initiative in the past. They will need encouragement and assurance when participating in the group.

Encourage Creative Concepts

"We tried that before and it didn't work." How many times have you heard that or "That is not the way we do it here." However, frequently, when the same idea is offered by a superior it will be taken seriously. Why not reverse the process so associates are listened to and encouraged to offer ideas. Of course they must be listened to and their ideas used or trust will evaporate. Why use their ideas? Establishing a culture of collaboration and creativity requires your staff feeling comfortable when sharing ideas based on their work experiences. Additionally, while research indicates a variety of generational differences, a common characteristic of every generation is the need to be heard and to have ideas used when developing solutions. Typically, those solutions are of much higher value.

The key to encouraging and supporting innovation within an organization involves the nature of a leader's ego. When encouraging new ideas, the good leader provides encouragement and recognition. Reassuring comments such as, "all ideas are good ideas," encourage new ideas and signal a welcoming sign that suggestions are welcome. The leader shines the spotlight on subordinates and recognizes extra effort. Doing so stimulates increased individual initiative and enhances leadership effectiveness. Encouraging new ideas also entails discouraging staff members from ridiculing or bullying colleagues who offer ideas. As a model, the leader refrains from ridicule and sarcasm.

When your group develops improvements that require participation by staff members in another department, your role as leader is to encourage your staff to communicate directly with staff of that department. Removing barriers by soliciting support from the department manager is important as well.

The general manager of an airline was walking through his operation one day and realized the storage of scrap metal was missing. When he asked the area supervisor he was told the mechanics knew of a vendor in another state who could use the scrap and suggested he be contacted. When they contacted him, the vendor agreed and paid $50,000 for the scrap. The general manager congratulated the supervisor for supporting new ideas and then congratulated the mechanics for taking initiative.

This same manager had plans to build a new test lab. He developed a plan for layout of the lab. However, upon reflection, he asked the lab technicians to design their own work space. Smiling, he observed later they had generated ideas he had not considered and the laboratory offices were much better organized. He celebrated their success by having a celebration in which all station personnel were invited to attend a new lab opening with a ribbon cutting.

The CEO of a leading software and IT networking company encourages new ideas by taking weekly walks through his operation with a food cart. As he passes through each department he asks associates to share ideas for improvement. When an associate offers an idea, he gives them something from the cart along with the authority to implement their idea. His executives have been constantly recruited by other companies but choose to remain because of their leader's willingness to listen to them and use their ideas. His company continues to innovate and remain competitive in its' market.

Reaching Consensus

A friend of mine discussed his frustration with his engineering group. They would discuss ideas for a project but it always seemed the person with the loudest voice and/or spoke with authority carried the decisions. Many of the engineers on his team were becoming frustrated and final designs were not working as desired. Their leader was not a facilitator he explained. Consensus occurs when all participants have been heard and everyone can "fully support" or at least "live with" the final plan. When all hands go up in agreement with and in support of the solution or plan you have consensus.

Creating the Environment

There is a difference between consensus and compromise yet the two are seen as the same in many organizations. Consensus means that every person involved in the decision supports the decision. Everyone wins. Compromise, on the other hand, creates winners and losers since majority vote carries the decision. In order to create an environment of consensus decisions, two factors must be considered.

A. It is important that everyone has an opportunity to speak and have confidence they can speak openly and truthfully without being criticized or punished.

Group Think is involved when there seems to be agreement among several members of the group so the other members go along in order to avoid conflict. The group loses out on ideas that could further enhance the conversation and decision and is cheated by those who fail to speak up. Utilizing the guidelines for brainstorming discussed earlier is a means for letting all group members know they will not be punished for speaking up and are encouraged to express their differing views on issues.

B. Everyone Owns the Decision when they leave the room. Consensus does not mean that everyone fully supports the final decision. It means that all ideas have been heard and people have been treated respectfully. It means that before the final vote everyone has agreed that they can fully support the solution or can live with it. If this cannot be accomplished a majority vote is the alternative.

A manager used to tell us he was fully engaged in building consensus. He would present a problem to his staff, give them his solution for solving the problem, and would then ask his staff to raise their hands in agreement! He would have truly been engaging his staff had he presented the problem, let them share ideas to solve it, facilitated them in selecting the best solution and checking to be certain everyone is in agreement. The steps for building consensus are listed below:

Steps for Reaching Consensus

1. **Establish criteria for the solution.**

   What are budgetary limits, does the group have the authority to implement their ideas, are there limited resources for the project and time constraints are examples of criteria to consider.

2. **Clean up the list of solutions.**

   There will be ideas that are very similar to others and can be combined. The facilitator should ask the group, "are these the same or are they different" when discussing eliminating duplicate ideas or combining similar ideas. If there is disagreement on whether two ideas are the same it is best to leave each separate and move on. This is also a good time for the facilitator to insure the group members have discussed and understand each of the ideas or solutions on the board.

3. **Make a new list.**

This is helpful if the list has become confusing as a result of the cleanup. If the list is understandable use the existing list. IF not make a new list for ease when voting.

4. **Vote on best solutions.**

Use the 80/20 rule for selecting best solutions. For example, if you have 30 solutions to consider, each group member would be allowed six selections (20 percent) on the list. The six solutions receiving the most tally marks, check marks or dots would be considered for the final decision.

5. **Discuss pros and cons of each solution.**

The facilitator's role is to review each of the six solutions asking the group members to discuss the advantages and disadvantages of each. This is also a good time to check out how each solution addresses the criteria established earlier.

6. **Discuss feelings about the solutions.**

Ask the group how they feel about the solutions they have selected. A reality test is to ask the group to raise their hands if they believe the solutions will solve the problem or address a market need. If everyone agrees you are working toward consensus. If a group member does not agree ask them why. Then ask the group how this person's concern can be included in the set of solutions being considered. This continues to build consensus and leads to better solutions.

7. **Final agreement on solutions.**

After discussing all alternatives for workable solutions the facilitator asks, "How many of you fully support or can live with this solution?" If all members raise their hands in agreement consensus has been reached. If not, consider further discussion of the solutions or using a majority vote instead.

8. **Action plan for implementing solutions.**

The solutions will be implemented to the extent the group takes action to do so. An action plan describing WHAT is to be done (solutions), WHO will implement each solution and WHEN each solution will be implemented increases the likelihood the solutions will be successfully implemented.

CHAPTER 9

Generate Great Decisions

The manner in which leaders make decisions creates the difference between managing individuals and leading collaborative and innovative enterprises. Furthermore, their ability to make decisions is the difference between making bad decisions or great decisions. In their book *Decisive*, Chip Heath and Dan Heath (2013) cite research indicating "four villains of decision making."

The first villain is "framing the decision too narrowly." For example, "How should we improve our healthcare delivery service" rather than "What do our patients need from us?"

The second villain of decision making is our tendency to pick a solution and find data that supports our idea. The authors, Heath and Heath, call it "confirmation bias." They refer to Dan Lovally, professor and decision-making researcher who said, "Confirmation bias is probably the single biggest problem in business, because even the most sophisticated people get it wrong. People go out and they're collecting the data, and they don't realize they're cooking the books." "When we want something to be true, we will spotlight the things that support it, and then, when we draw conclusions from those spotlighted scenes, we'll congratulate ourselves on a reasoned decision. Oops!"

When buying or selling a house I used to pick the real estate company with the most appealing signs. More recently, I have avoided confirmation bias by using a decision-making process. Three real estate firms are invited to see the house and design a strategy for marketing and selling the property. The agent who provides a strategy tailored to my house and the local market is awarded the listing. I also include in the decision-making process anyone who is a stakeholder in the project. Houses have sold sooner and at a more satisfying price since changing my process.

The third villain of decision making is "short-term emotion." Even when we know what we must do our emotional ties will influence our decision. How many times have you seen someone pick their favorite team to win a contest knowing it faces overwhelming odds. Or, how often do we see a political candidate win a contest while offering policy considerations that have failed time and time again in the past. The decision to pick a certain team or candidate is based on how we feel emotionally about the situation. Facts just get in the way! The authors offer a solution. Ask what a stranger coming into the situation would say. Your answer will help cut through the emotional tangles being faced.

The fourth villain of decision making is "overconfidence." "People think they know more than they do about how the future will unfold."

Heath and Heath reported a study revealing that when doctors reckoned themselves "completely certain" about a diagnosis, they were wrong 40 percent of the time. When students made estimates that they believed had only a 1 percent chance of being wrong they were actually wrong 27 percent of the time. We are challenged in that our crystal balls seen to have lost their glow and our past performances may not provide the data desired for future decisions.

The ability to make better decisions involves a structure and process that provides for inclusiveness and deliberation. A leader recently observed that he uses all four decision styles based on generational differences. The four alternatives for making business or family decisions include the following:

Leader Directed

The leader makes all decisions, discusses issues, and plans individually with members in his/her office. Information is provided on a "need to know" basis (Figure 9.1).

This decision-making style is prevalent in traditionally managed organizations. These companies manage individuals and overlook the power of developing individuals and leading collaborative work groups. The current emission control violations experienced by Volkswagen have been attributed to a Leader Focused structure of decision making. In fact, recently in a business news report, an observer noted this form of management used by Volkswagen discourages innovation.

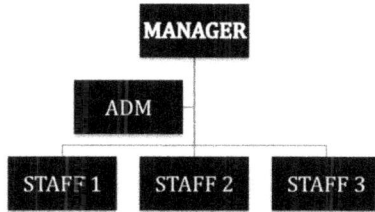

Figure 9.1 Leader directed model

There are situations in which this Command decision-making approach should be utilized. It has application when there is an emergency and decisions need to be made quickly or the leader is the only person with the knowledge to make the decision. For example, a storm is coming, and the department needs to evacuate or a client has announced they will be coming the following day to audit how work is performed.

The advantage of using this approach is it is quick and satisfies the manager. The disadvantage is it fails to solicit the input of staff members and creates dependency on the leader. It stifles input, creativity, and initiative among group members. Without participation by work group members, the probability of successful implementation of any initiative is unlikely. In a collaborative culture, the Command style of decision making is typically used approximately 10 percent of the time.

The Superintendent of a production facility had been using this style of decision making for most of his career. He made a presentation in a management meeting regarding how he and his organization had changed. "I got so tired of everyone asking me to get tape from the cabinet for them!" he laughed. "I was ready to retire," he added. "Now I delegate and they get their own tape. Furthermore, when they leave the plant at night they are not laughing and horsing around like they did in the past. Now, when they leave, they are talking about their work. I have decided not to retire for a few more years and now have supper with my wife," he said with a smile.

Group Involved

The Group Involved (Figure 9.2) approach to decision making is used to gather facts and data in order to make better informed decisions. It becomes the predominant form of decision making as managers shift from Leader Directed decisions.

Group Involved

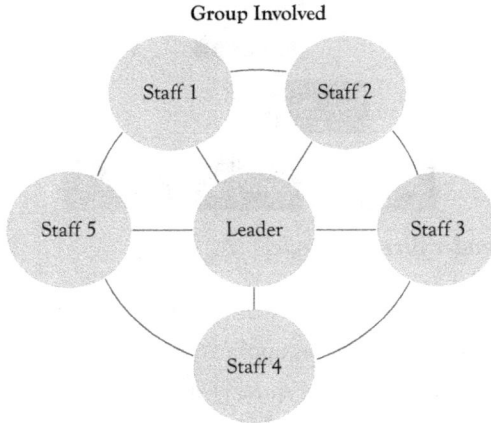

Figure 9.2 Group involved model

The manager facilitates group problem solving and improving work processes and service delivery. The manager still makes the final decision after receiving ideas and data from work group members.

For example, before making the decision on clients who are coming the following day for an audit, the manager would call a staff meeting, inform staff of the situation, and solicit their ideas on how to proceed. The manager would then decide on the final action plan and proceed with assistance of staff members. A client began using this approach in staff meetings. He asked his profit center team for ideas to reduce labor and utility costs. After hearing their ideas he agreed, asked them to implement those ideas and report to him as they progressed. The following month his profit center had the lowest budget costs of the 10 profit center groups.

There is a caution when soliciting input from staff. Recently, someone described how their company uses this approach. She and other staff members were asked to recommend a new location for their branch office. The manager made the final decision, disregarding their recommendations and choosing another location. Not only were their ideas not used, they received no feedback about the reasoning for the final decision. This may have been convenient for the manager but was certainly not best for staff or customers.

Be sure to use staff ideas or inform them why their ideas were not used. Trust erodes if staff members offer ideas that are ignored. They will trust and contribute when they see their ideas being used or are given honest reasons for not using those ideas.

Group Collaboration

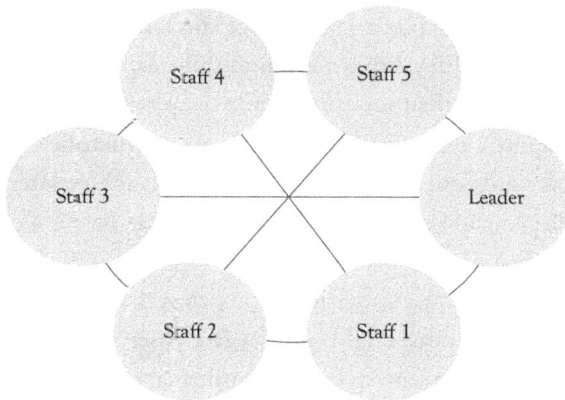

Figure 9.3 Group collaboration model

The advantage to this approach is it is a fast and flexible way to generates data and facts for more informed decisions. Staff members feel good about being involved and having a voice in how work is performed. The likelihood of successful implementation of ideas and solutions is enhanced as a result. The disadvantage is members feel betrayed if their ideas are not used and will be reluctant to respond to future inquiries.

Group Collaboration

This approach to making decisions is used when decisions affect the whole group and when the group is responsible for creating and implementing concepts they have developed (Figure 9.3). Responsibilities would include improving or reengineering work processes, product quality, new product development, and introduction and problem solving customer/ supplier issues. The manager becomes one vote within the work group. Other group members are asked to facilitate brainstorming and decision making. Decisions are typically made using consensus.

A small business owner used this decision-making style to become more competitive in her market. Over the last few years, her restaurant had lost revenue as other restaurants moved into the area. She invited her crew to meet with her one morning. They brainstormed how to increase revenues and developed a game plan for doing so. This owner chose to be one vote in the final decision and together she with the whole staff implemented their ideas to increase revenue.

Since increasing customer counts had become challenging, the staff decided to focus on increasing the average check of each customer dining in their restaurant. They reorganized into shift teams and along with the owner implemented their ideas for improving services and products. The following month's revenues (check average) had increased significantly and so did for subsequent months. The owner's daughter, attending community college, made a presentation on their initiative for a class project and won the first place.

The advantage of this leadership approach is the greater commitment obtained for shared ideas. Higher quality fact-based decisions were made. Higher quality and improved work performance resulted. The disadvantage is the greater amount of time required for making group decisions.

Group Empowered

This method of decision making is used when the work group has the knowledge and information to make decisions. Group Collaboration and Group Empowered are the dominant decision-making processes when developing a collaborative culture for achieving higher levels of success (Figure 9.4).

The leader has developed a creative engine by delegating key responsibilities and decisions to the work group. Design and implementation tasks and decisions are assigned to the group. The group chooses a team leader and becomes fully responsible for hiring new members, correcting

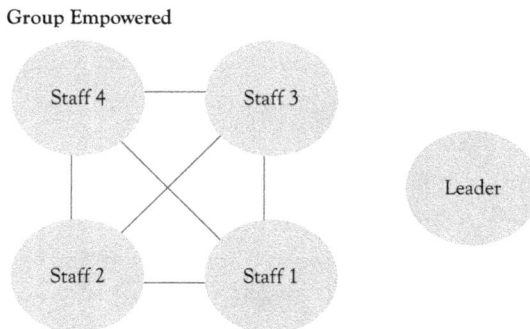

Figure 9.4 Group empowered model

behavior, conducting research, and creating new products and services to continually move the organization forward.

The leader becomes a resource provider, buffer, removes obstacles getting in the way of project initiatives, and serves as liaison with senior management. The work and decisions are strategic in nature as products and services designed are defined during the strategic planning process. Many of these same people were engaged in goal setting and task development ensuring all initiatives are aligned with the strategy of your enterprise. Everyone begins with the end in mind!

Delegation is a process in which a leader develops a customer chain from top to bottom of the organization. Each level is the client of the level above and is empowered to exceed the expectations of their internal clients. Those who deal directly with external customers are empowered to make changes in the way work is performed and to enhance products and services.

Delegation has a lot to do with your management philosophy. Some leaders believe that people will only do the minimum to get by while others believe that for the most part people want to do their best and will do so if they know what is expected. For leaders who question the motivation of staff, a concern is usually expressed that should they delegate their department will get out of control and they will risk looking bad to their superiors.

I have found just the opposite to be the case. When I served as Director of Human Resources for a software company, I decided to improve performance within our department. My first action was to become clear with everyone regarding our vision and mission for serving the internal customers of our company. We then began cross-training so that employment knew benefit administration, training knew how to recruit, and benefit administration learned the basics of salary administration. After I felt they were capable of supporting each other and I had seen evidence of their cooperation in our weekly meetings, I decided to try the big test. They were informed that I would be on vacation for two weeks and each was provided signing authority for their area of responsibility. I informed them my desk would be clear when I left and I wanted my desk to be clear when I returned from vacation.

Two weeks later, I returned to work. There was absolutely nothing on my desk. It looked just like it did the day I left. I was horrified. I realized they were becoming self-managing and delegation worked well with them. The result was a total change in my responsibilities to walking around visiting with each executive and attending departmental meetings. I was able to inform our team in our weekly meetings of impending personnel issues and we were prepared to help when asked to do so.

Several benefits resulted from the changes. Our department became more creative and innovative. We reduced recruiting wait times and began providing benefits to our employees that were much less costly but added value to their lives. Additionally, each of us could help a client if our specialist was out of the office which reduced wait times and increased customer satisfaction.

In order to delegate, several factors should be considered. The leader must be prepared to turn over responsibility for decision making and problem solving to the individual or work group. The individual or group should have the skills and knowledge to accept the responsibility, make good decisions, and use problem solving to accomplish their tasks and goals. Many of the leaders I work with tell me their group is not ready because they do not have the knowledge or skills to handle new tasks. Usually, a work group lacks skills and knowledge because the leader is operating in the Directive style and is rewarded by handling everything themselves while appearing very busy. The leader may also believe people will do only the minimum required.

An effective leader determines skill sets required of staff and provides skill development training and cross-training for associates. Staff can then be authorized to accept more responsibility and make more decisions. For example, groups could manage their own budgets, make purchases within defined boundaries, decide on staff assignments, participate in the hiring process, and choosing new group members. Leaders can provide many opportunities to delegate and innovate based on their choice of decision-making styles and assumptions about people.

Engaging those closest to the work keeps the organization moving ahead as new ideas are created, work performance increases and solutions resolve vexing problems.

A plant manager was experiencing excessive material costs. His budget had mushroomed to $250,000 per year. He met with his mechanics and machine operators and assigned supervision of supplies to them. Each group was supplied a storage area for their tools and provided security locks for their supply units. Each unit team developed a material supply budget for the upcoming coming year. The budget totaled $100,000. Throughout the year, the groups supervised their supplies and ordered only as needed. The year-end budget reported total plant material expense of $50,000. These mechanics and machine operators managed to reduce material costs over $200,000 per year. Their leader trusted them and they returned that trust.

A strategy to implement a new service was undertaken by another client. The challenge was to implement a breakfast buffet in every restaurant in their region. A cross-functional team was assembled and empowered to

Collaborative Survey					
Behavior	No 1	Poor 2	Adequate 3	Good 4	Very Good 5
Leader takes responsibility for mistakes.					
Leader sees problems as opportunities.					
Leader speaks calmly and without anger.					
Leader encourages us to come up with new ideas.					
Leader recognizes us for our ideas.					
Leader rewards us for new ideas that are used.					
Leader facilitates our meetings using a flipchart with free-wheeling and round-robin brainstorming.					
Leader leads us to consensus (win-win) decisions.					
Many decisions are delegated to our work group.					
We speak 80% of the time and leader speaks 20% of the time in our meetings.					
We are trained and use problem solving and consensus decision-making tools.					

Figure 9.5 Collaborative survey

develop an implementation plan and execute the plan. They met regularly and developed a scorecard and goals aligned with their strategy. Over subsequent months, the buffet was implemented one profit center after another until every restaurant in the region offered buffet breakfasts. Of 40 regions, this region was the only region to completely implement the corporate challenge.

The advantage to moving your enterprise into a creative engine is clear. Products and services are typically developed faster and with higher levels of quality as everyone learns from their successes and mistakes (Figure 9.5).

Plan of Action

Use the chart shown in Figure 9.6 to develop a plan of action for increasing collaboration in your enterprise. After discussing your survey, decide new behaviors that could create a collaborative culture and list those behaviors under the START column. Then, list those behaviors that should be stopped under the column START and behaviors to maintain under CONTINUE.

Start	Stop	Continue

Figure 9.6 Action plan

MOTIVATE

"If you're good to your staff when things are going well, they'll rally when times go bad."

—Mary Kay Ash

"We are all motivated by a keen desire for praise, and the better a man is, the more he is inspired by glory."

—Cicero

CHAPTER 10

Think Positively

Leadership behaviors required for motivating the workforce include celebrating improvements and goal attainment, positive thinking, calmly correcting behavior, and being flexible in leadership styles with associates.

Thinking positively does not mean you avoid discussing and dealing with unpleasant situations and problems. It is the issue of the glass being half full or half empty. I know a leader who approaches each problem with gusto because she believes the problem will lead to a greater opportunity. I know another who tends to avoid confronting problems because he believes the problem will only get worse if it is addressed. Clearly, the leader who sees the glass half empty person gets much less accomplished than the one who sees the glass half full! However, being positive should never be equated with being unrealistic.

Positive thinking is the act of approaching each day as a great day to be alive and being of service. This leader smiles and laughs with associates and when a person makes a mistake asks them what they learned in the process. Positive thinking does not include the behaviors of being sarcastic to be funny or joking in such a way as to make someone feel bad in front of others. I watched a basketball coach yell to a player on the court "Stupid!" For the rest of the half, the player turned to the bench after every play to check the coach's reaction so as to avoid being yelled at again. Another coach after a tough loss commented on how well his team played. It was obvious the players appreciated the respect shown them. It is the same in business. When a leader observes how well someone tried rather than offering threats, people try harder. When they are punished by ridicule or harsh words and tone of voice, they attempt to avoid the leaders displeasure by doing only what is asked to avoid further punishment.

A leader who thinks positively is the one who greets staff warmly, sending the message they are important. When the group or individual misses deadlines, the leader shows understanding and uses problem solving to get back on track. One of the finest examples I can think of is a story told about the respected basketball coach, Dean Smith, well known for the innovations he contributed to basketball. As the story goes, one day at practice one of his big men was out of position on a play. The play, however, resulted in a score. Coach Smith stopped practice to discuss what the team had learned. They created a new play out of this mistake integrating it into their practice sessions and playbook. Any coach or business leader using positive thinking will use mistakes as a catalyst for innovation just as Dean Smith did.

Positive thinking also involves you catching people doing right as well as people doing wrong. Certainly, people need feedback and correcting when they make errors but they also need to hear when they have done well and corrected their mistakes.

Celebrate Improvement and Goal Attainment

Many supervisors think they are showing weakness by expressing appreciation for work performed. As a manager once told me "they know I approve because I don't say anything to them unless someone screws up." However, studies and experience demonstrate that leaders who acknowledge desired performance typically achieve higher levels of individual and group initiative and creativity.

There are several considerations when deciding on celebration and goal setting procedures.

Influences on Work Behavior

Business owners and managers tend to experience frustration managing their personnel. Some of the comments I have heard, and you probably have heard also, including the following:

"People just want to get by these days. Why should I pay them more than minimum wage?" No doubt there are some people who are interested in getting a paycheck and doing as little as possible. However, for many others, the issue may be more about how they are treated at work or the lack of systems in place for motivating them to do more. The good news is there are systems and leadership behaviors that can be used to encourage personnel to do more than just get by. Those systems include both feedback and recognition systems combined with the leadership behaviors of positive thinking and catching people doing well.

"People here don't take initiative." While this can be true for many people in many organizations, the reason may be more than the person's willingness to take initiative. Having goals aligned with the organization's strategy, combined with feedback systems on current and desired performance tend to minimize this issue while increasing initiative and innovation.

"Why can't they just come to work and do their jobs?" Managers have expressed this sentiment over the years. The question could more aptly be "why do they have me managing people?" Management at its best can be frustrating; however, with proper training of both leaders and personnel, a greater probability exists that your personnel will come to work and do their jobs well.

"Our employees don't seem to care." For many people, the issues are more about what they encountered in past work experiences. They may have been overlooked for promotions, been punished unfairly, or may have been ignored or overlooked. These experiences may influence their actions when working with you. Personnel with such experiences can be engaged and motivated once again when using objective feedback and positive reinforcement systems throughout the organization and personalized reinforcement with individuals.

Why We Do the Things We Do

It can be helpful to understand what directs our behavior. Why do we work for the companies we work for, why do we do the work we do, why do we come to work every day, or why do we avoid work altogether. There are reasons why we behave the way we do. Those reasons are described in the ABC model.

ABC Model

Research of human behavior has identified causes and effects on our behavior whether at home or at work. We do what we do because of what happens when we do it. Behavior is a function of consequences to our behavior. For example, I like to run and was encouraged to run a half-marathon in large part because of the positive comments and interest shown me by the recreation center staff. I also had a goal to put a 13.1 sticker on my truck. The encouragement was key to continuing my running behavior. But something started me thinking about this run. It was a challenge by my daughter for me to get in shape and run with her in a half-marathon. So with a prompt from my daughter to begin training and the encouragement of the Recreation Center staff after each training session, I successfully completed the race. My truck has a 13.1 sticker on the back window!

This story illustrates the key elements of the ABC model. Our behavior first needs a prompt. This prompt is called an Activator. It prompts behavior. My daughter challenging me to run with her was a prompt, an Activator. It started my workout behavior. However, for me to continue my training for this long run, I needed much encouragement. That encouragement is referred to as Positive Consequences. The positive encouragement from recreation staff along with my setting goals with staff maintained and increased my training runs from 15 miles per week to 27 miles per week.

The illustration in Figure 10.1 is designed to show the relationship among Activators, Behavior, and Consequences. In this illustration, consequences are shown to become activators. For example, staff encouragement and interest after each run strengthened my running behavior and prompted my next run.

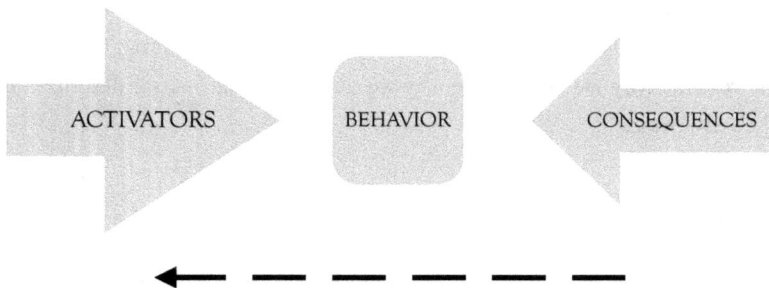

Figure 10.1 ABC Model

Activators

As we have discussed, activators start or prompt our behavior and are used in many organizational systems. Three considerations regarding activators are as follows:

1. Activators happen **before** a behavior occurs such as persons, places, things, or events.
2. Activators provide a trigger to **prompt** a behavior.
3. Activators **do not** cause a behavior to continually occur.

Examples of Activators

Objectives	Deadlines	Manuals
Training	Speeches	Policies
Instructions	Feedback	Signs
Requests	Performance	Reviews

Most managers rely on requests or instructions when directing staff to initiate or complete tasks. Asking an employee several times to perform a task is referred to as "over activating" or in planer language "nagging." Traditionally, there is much reliance by managers on activators to motivate behavior. Activators are important for developing and directing behavior. However, relying solely on activators results in minimal success.

Behavior

To assist clients to understand what behavior is and is not, I ask participants to describe the behaviors associated with the following terms:

1. Bad attitude
2. Lazy worker
3. Unmotivated person
4. Under performer

Normally, the class learns that the same behaviors apply to all four descriptors. They agree using such general terms will not communicate to an employee or team what is required to be corrected or changed.

In order to guide personnel, 21st-century leaders must focus on pinpointed behavior. Pinpointed behaviors are:

- **Observable.** The behavior must be seen. For example, we see someone coming to work late. We are not able to see what they think about arriving late and we do not know how they feel about it. We do not know their attitude but we do know they arrived late.
- **Measurable.** In order to influence and change behavior we must be able to measure the behavior. In the example above, we can count the number of days each week this person arrives late and we can count the amount of time this person has been late.
- **Reliable.** Reliable means that two or more people can see the behavior and agree on the number of times it occurs. For example, all staff members in the office could see when this person comes and count either the number of times he is late in a week or month or the elapsed amount time missed at work.

Managers are not responsible for internal behaviors such as thoughts, feelings, motives, and attitudes. You are only responsible for observable, pinpointed behaviors.

Consequences of Our Actions

Consequences are defined as actions that:

A. **Come after** the behavior and influence our behavior. For example, it is a work day and the weather is bad. You know people will be staying home and you probably should also. However, you look at a list of the things you must accomplish so you bundle up and go to the office. Hardly anyone is at work and you are getting lots done when someone walks by and says, "It is great to see you and nice to have you around today." In this example, you were prompted to go to the office after looking at your list. You experienced the consequences of getting a lot accomplished and receiving praise. Consequences come after behavior.

B. **Produced by** the behavior. Consequences occur as a result of what we do. For example, I am driving down a slippery slope and my truck begins to slide. I experience the consequence of feeling out of control and experiencing high anxiety. That feeling of anxiety is the result of driving and sliding. The consequence was produced by the behavior.

C. **Strengthen or weaken** the behavior. If we like what happens to us we will do it again. If we do not we will stop doing it. In the earlier example, if the person coming in to work late continues to do so without cost, he is receiving positive consequences for late behavior. If he is given feedback and stops coming in late, he has received punishing consequences and the behavior has stopped.

Types of Consequences

Punishment is produced by behavior, weakens or stops behavior, teaches avoidance, produces compliance, creates negative side effects, and the employee gets something she/he does not want. It has the effect of stopping behavior completely but only temporarily. We know someone has been punished by observing their actions. If their behavior stops they have been punished (Figure 10.2).

Many times the punishment must be repeated to continue discouraging the same behaviors. How many times have you heard a manager say, "I have corrected him time and time again?"

I once served a carpet manufacturing company in middle Georgia. The company produced a high quality carpet and enforced stringent rules for producing quality and minimizing waste. A part of the enforcement

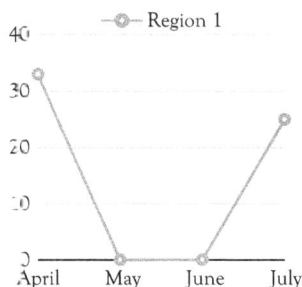

Figure 10.2 Punishment effect

was assigning operators time off without pay based on yards of carpet produced with defects. One fall morning, a week before deer hunting season opened, an operator approached his supervisor and said, "How many yards of carpet do I have to screw up to get a whole week off?" Punishment can be hard to apply and as you have seen from several examples can have an opposite effect from the one desired.

I know of few companies who effectively use progressive discipline as punishment to stop behavior. One client began using the process with verbal warning, written warning, second written warning, and termination effectively when they began applying each step of the process quickly after the behavior. For example, if someone was late to work and did not call, the process was initiated the same day. Employees saw the impact after several warnings and knew their late behavior would be punished. Coming to work late stopped.

Positive reinforcement is produced by the behavior, maintains or strengthens behavior, the person gets something they want, performance is optimized, and side effects are usually positive. It strengthens behavior. We know whether someone is being reinforced by the person's reactions. If their behavior continues or increases their behavior is being positively reinforced (Figure 10.3).

Several years ago we consulted with a production company. At their warehouse receiving dock, a truck driver had earned quite a reputation. The receiving department management issued warning slips to drivers who hit the loading dock when backing up. This punishment was designed to encourage drivers to be careful and avoid damaging the dock.

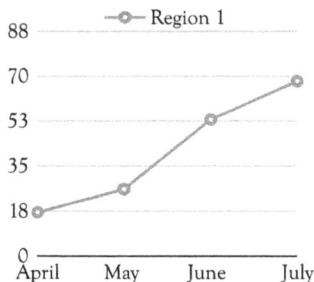

Figure 10.3 Reinforcement effect

However, this remedy was having the opposite effect with a certain truck driver. Every time he approached the dock, everyone in the receiving area would come out to watch. Sure enough, he would hit the dock. Everyone cheered as the manager came out to issue another warning slip, setting new records each time for this trucker. The trucker left the facility smiling. While warehouse management was attempting to stop trucks hitting the dock, the punishment had become positive reinforcement for this truck driver. We know his behavior was being reinforced because he continued hitting the dock. His dock hitting behavior was being maintained and strengthened by warehouse management.

CHAPTER 11

Managing Consequences

In the example describing punishment and punishment systems, as well as positive reinforcement and reinforcement systems, several reasons exist for why these systems are not as effective as the organization would wish. The reasons include the **type** of consequence being used, the **timing** of the consequence, and the **probability** the consequence will occur.

Type of Consequence

- **Positive**—as perceived by employee. The consequence, positive reinforcement, is seen as desirable to the employee and their behavior improves.
- **Negative**—as perceived by employee. The consequence, punishment, is seen as undesirable by the employee and their behavior stops.

Timing of Consequence

- **Immediate**—while the behavior is occurring or immediately afterward.
- **Future**—any delay, the longer the delay the less impact the consequence has on behavior.

Probability the Consequence Will Occur

- **Certain**—always follows the behavior. Consequences are promised, and the employee can count on receiving the consequence after their task is completed.

Effectiveness Of Consequences On Behavior		
Highly effective	Positive, immediate, certain (PIC)	Negative, immediate, certain (NIC)
Moderately effective	Positive, future, certain (PFC)	Negative, future, certain (PFC)
Low effectiveness	Positive, future, uncertain (PFU)	Negative, future, uncertain (NFU)

Figure 11.1 PIC/NIC model

- **Uncertain**—may or may not follow the behavior. Consequences are promised but sometimes happen and other times do not happen.

Using the criteria above, we can evaluate the effectiveness of any consequence or systematic application of consequences in the workplace. The chart in Figure 11.1 outlines the relationship between these factors and the effectiveness of any system of consequences.

Evaluate Impact of Consequences

Enter in the boxes to the right first, is the consequence positive or negative (P/N); second box, is the consequence delivered immediately or in future (I/F), and third box, is the consequence certain to occur or uncertain to occur (C/U). For example, in the first situation, slicing fruit, N would be written in first box, I would be in the second box, and U would be written in the third box (Figure 11.2).

After completing this exercise you may understand why many systems used in organizations experience limited effectiveness or are completely ineffective! The example discussed earlier of the company effectively using punishment considered its impact on behavior. Originally, assessment of their system of punishment was NFU as with most companies. The management was trained and committed to changing their system to NIC with resulting success.

We have defined and reviewed the impact on behavior of both punishment and positive reinforcement. Because punishment is difficult to use and works for a short time, it is helpful to understand how to optimize positive reinforcement (PIC) to motivate and innovate.

Behavior	Consequence	P/N	I/F	C/U
1. Slicing fruit toward you	Knife slips and cuts hand	N	I	U
2. Employee comes to work early and never misses a day	At annual review she gets compliment and letter to file			
3. Employee makes negative comments to coworkers	Gets corrective feedback after several people complain			
4. Employee is tardy	Sometimes he is asked to arrive on time			
5. Employee continually produces work with multiple errors	Gets verbal reprimand when supervisor gets aggravated			

Figure 11.2 Consequence eval tool

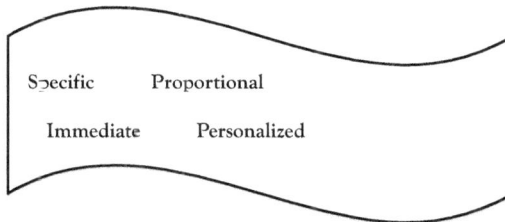

Figure 11.3 Reinforcement guidelines

Using Positive Reinforcement

Tangible positive reinforcement: This is something we can touch, see, and feel and usually costs money. For example, providing pizzas to celebrate meeting a milestone would be a tangible form of positive reinforcement. A magazine subscription or trip paid by the company serves as other examples.

Intangible positive reinforcement: This is something that does not cost money and is written or verbal in nature. For example, sending someone a text message or note thanking him/her for help on the project would be an intangible form of positive reinforcement. Recently, someone recognized their electrician on Facebook for help at their home.

Guidelines: The guidelines for using positive reinforcement apply to both tangible and intangible forms of reinforcement (Figure 11.3).

- **Specific**
  To be effective, the individual and/or team should know exactly
  why they are receiving positive reinforcement. Otherwise,
  they will not know what you want and may not continue
  the behaviors you intended to maintain or increase. This also
  means your reinforcement is contingent on specific behaviors.
  If you cannot explain clearly and specifically why you are
  recognizing an individual or your team you risk reinforcing
  alternative behaviors. If coffee and bagels are provided one
  morning at work use the time to thank the group for meeting
  their goals on time, or reducing the time taken to serve clients
  as examples. Be certain **not to say,** "this is to thank you for
  your hard work." They have no idea what they have done to
  please you or meet expectations with such an explanation.

- **Immediate**
  Reinforcement is produced by the behavior. For that reason,
  it is critical to recognize an achievement as close to the
  activity as possible in order for it to be effective. A director of
  consulting had developed a solution for his consulting team.
  He bought tickets for events such as plays, sporting events,
  symphony performances, and movies and kept these tickets
  in his desk drawer. He would usually know from clients who
  had done exceptional work installing software that week.
  When his consultants would come into his office to debrief,
  he would pull out tickets from his desk and hand them to
  consultants receiving customer compliments. He explained
  that in the past he would obtain something for reinforcement
  after talking with his team. The time delay made it difficult
  for him to align performance with the reinforcement he
  explained. This new arrangement gives him the ability to
  reinforce as immediately as possible.

- **Personalized**
  Several years ago I was flying to see a client. The person sitting
  next to me was reading a magazine and we began talking
  as she put the magazine aside. She was on vacation after
  completing a major project having demanding time lines and

problems to solve. She told me her boss called her in before leaving on this vacation and handed her the latest edition of the Harvard Business Review (HBR). She was given a two-year subscription to show appreciation for her achievements. She explained that the vacation, paid by the company, was nice but what she appreciated most was her boss taking the time to learn about her and how much she enjoyed HBR.

- **Proportional**
  This means the reward is in relation to the magnitude of the performance being required. For example, the director of consulting provided tickets with various levels of value to recognize various levels of achievement. The project manager who worked long days and weekends to bring in a demanding project on time received company paid vacation. The group described earlier who innovated the construction process and the facility designs was promised a trip to Hawaii if they met their challenging goal. The achievement meant greater market dominance and the reinforcement was in proportion to their achievement.

Understanding what motivates people is important for creating an innovative culture. It is based on the premise that people will do what you want them to do as long as they know your expectations and are recognized for their efforts. Every generation has similar expectations. If you challenge your staff to collaborate and create new ways to produce a product, they should know their extra efforts will be recognized. Additionally, if we want to complete new initiatives and establish a culture of collaboration and creativity, it is imperative we do so.

Feedback, Telling It Like It Is

The CEO of a Fortune 50 company recently explained the secret to her success was overcoming the reluctance of giving bad news. She became more successful when she began "telling it like it is." Feedback is a way of providing both the good and the bad news. It is information provided about past performance that guides future performance. Any leader's success is tied in large part to the manner and frequency of feedback provided to his/her team. If the leader is guiding a project consisting of team members representing all areas of the enterprise, it will be important that project members are provided frequent feedback to guide them and maintain their participation on the project. If this is a permanent work group or individual, the same principle applies as well.

Effective Feedback

Feedback can be positive, it can be negative, it can be verbal or written, and can be represented by data on charts and graphs. For an organization to innovate, it is critical that everyone be fully informed about their individual performance, their work group's performance, and their organization's performance. Several considerations are important to keep in mind when establishing feedback systems (Figure 11.4).

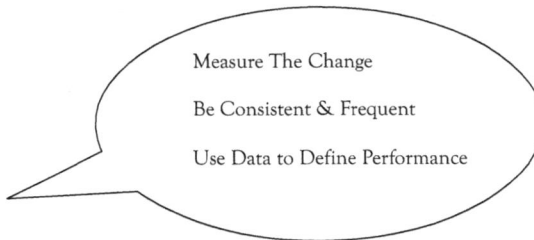

Measure The Change

Be Consistent & Frequent

Use Data to Define Performance

Figure 11.4 Measurement

- **You can't change what you can't measure.**
  In other words, if you wish to change the way a health care emergency room (ER) operates, it is important to collect data that measure ER performance. If your strategy is to create an integrated healthcare model, data should be collected that measure the innovations required to create the new model. For example, the percent completion of a project plan could be a measure, revenue income during the change and afterward, the number of integrated services developed and implemented, and patient wellness measures could be considered based on the goals of the organizations strategy.

- **Be consistent and frequent.**

  Data-based feedback and personal verbal feedback needs to
  be provided on a regular basis. The Manage by Exception
  philosophy will not work to improve performance around
  innovation of any sort. Plot data weekly in order to have the
  most impact on performance directed toward monthly goal
  achievement.

  If the people doing the work learn how they are performing
  at month's end, they have no chance to affect the data and
  accomplish their goals. On the other hand, if members of the
  work group know their progress daily and weekly they have a
  much better chance of modifying their work in order to attain
  monthly goals. Golfers do not wait to count their strokes
  when they get in the clubhouse, baseball teams don't wait to
  calculate the score at the end of the game. In both examples,
  the performers know how they are doing after every effort to
  perform. The same consistency and frequency applies to any
  organization's strategy for innovation and market dominance.

- **Define performance using data.**

  People don't argue with their own data. Discuss with your
  group what performance data would be most meaningful
  to them. There is also the matter of control. They may feel
  like they can control some data but not other. For example,
  they can't control enterprise wide product design initiatives.
  But they may control wasted time and materials and the
  assembly process for new products coming on line. Encourage
  associates to collect and graph the data along with setting
  goals and sub goals for improvement.

     People own the data they collect and review. I worked
  with a client not long ago and took them on a benchmarking
  trip to visit a company that had implemented Kaizen.
  Each department had graphs posted on their outside walls
  highlighting key performance goals. The manager of each
  department presented their charts. I learned later the
  managers decided on the data and performance to be graphed
  and updated the charts in order for them to look consistent

and present well. Department employees had no participation in decision making or graph development and had little interest or ownership in the outcomes.

Positive feedback: This is the feedback on past performance that shows approval of the performance. If someone or the group has improved turnaround time in their department, positive feedback might come in the form of a letter from the director, a note on charts posted in the work area recording turnaround time or it could be provided during a team meeting. As part of their lean initiative, a real estate department was merged with construction project managers and organized into cross-functional work groups aligned with geographical areas of their market. Each week each geographic subgroup met to review activities and their performance charts. Each month the whole group met, reviewed performance charts measuring total group performance noted individual contributions, and celebrated their progress by having lunch together.

These groups working in their silos in past years had never build more than seven units in a year. The following year, working together with a clear focus and frequent feedback they produced more than 20 units. These groups innovated the manner in which work was performed and the design of units being built resulting in greater dominance of their marketplace.

Negative feedback: This is the feedback on past performance communicating disapproval of the performance. Please note, it conveys disapproval of performance not disapproval of the person. Data-based feedback facilitates the communication of such performance. For example, rather than the coach we described earlier shouting "Stupid" he might have shouted instead, three turnovers! A maintenance manager in a hospital was having difficulty getting department personnel to complete a service request form. They would just come by and ask for help. One day he greeted them holding a golf counter. If they did not submit a work request he held up the counter and clicked it. "What is that," they would ask. "I am just counting," he would say. Within a week, everyone provided work orders when requesting assistance.

Verbal feedback: This is provided for both positive and negative feedback. As discussed earlier, such feedback should happen immediately after the person's behavior and be corrected or recognized accordingly.

Many times the only feedback needed is the performance count. For example, a supervisor was frustrated with an employee frequently arriving to work late. One Monday morning, he stood by the front door and when the employee entered late the supervisor said, "one." The following day he was at the door and when the employee came in late he said, "two." The following day the employee came to work on time and the supervisor said, "one" and began a new count for on time behavior.

Visual feedback: We discussed earlier the importance of posting charts reflecting performance toward goals. The chart in Figure 11.5 illustrates a creative way a Head Nurse used to increase punctuality of her staff.

	1/7	1/14	1/21	1/28	2/7	2/14	2/21	2/28
WEEK ENDING								
Jean	★	★	●	★	★	★	●	★
Lisa	●	★	★	★	★	★	★	★
Hannah	●	●	★	★	★	★	★	★

Figure 11.5 Feedback system

My client explained that she had given verbal warnings and written warnings to no avail and did not know what to do. I suggested she take positive measures since punishment was not making needed changes. After some discussions, she engaged her staff in designing a feedback chart and symbols.

The nursing staff designed the chart, picked symbols to indicate punctual or late behavior and agreed to post it in their lunchroom. Staff members volunteered to update the chart each week. The staff and Head Nurse determined positive reinforcement for accomplishing their goals. Their reinforcement was having lunch together every month they achieved their goal of 100 percent.

January was baseline data before they initiated their project. In February, the department began experiencing 100 percent of staff coming to work on time with the additional benefit of 100 percent attendance. The department maintained higher levels of performance and improved patient satisfaction for the rest of the year as the Head Nurse practiced Positive Thinking and Celebrating Success.

Do's and Don'ts

Earlier in this section, we discussed guidelines for giving feedback. Of critical importance is being **Specific** by using measures of performance. Providing the feedback as **Immediate** as possible is also critical to the effectiveness of your feedback. There are two other considerations worth considering:

1. **Do not mix positive feedback with negative feedback.**

   When an employee hears you tell them something nice and then spends the rest of the conversation giving negative feedback, imagine what the employee will be thinking the next time you offer positive feedback. She will not hear the positive as she considers what she did wrong waiting for the negative feedback to follow. Some training tells managers offer comments to make the person feel good before correcting them. This advice makes the manager feel better but does not help the relationship with the employee. The only time to mix positive and negative feedback is either when the employee is in training or receiving annual performance reviews.

2. **Four to one feedback.**

   Several years ago, a management magazine reported research indicating the highest performing and creative organizations experienced a ratio of 3.95 times more positive feedback than negative feedback. The ratio was rounded up to 4 to 1. Other data indicated the ratio in human service organizations to be even higher, 5 to 1. Using positive feedback to catch people doing good works is the backbone of creating a positive culture encouraging risk taking for greater levels of creativity and innovation.

Assignment

Develop and implement a plan to improve performance in your program (Figure 11.6).

Performance Improvement Plan for: (Name of Person)
Individual Behavior:_____(Specific Behavior)
Goal:_____ (Goal for Personal Improvement)

Calmly Correct in Private

Praise in public and correct in private is a message we all hear. Yet it tends to be overlooked more times than not in many organizations.

I watched a true leader who calmly smiled while asking an employee why the error occurred and what the employee might do to correct the situation. The employee responded and left feeling intact and feeling motivated to perform better for someone who showed trust in her.

Plan	Completion Date
1. Behavior/Goal	
2. Measure (data)	
3. Feedback frequency	
4. Reinforcement plan	

Figure 11.6 Behavior improvement plan

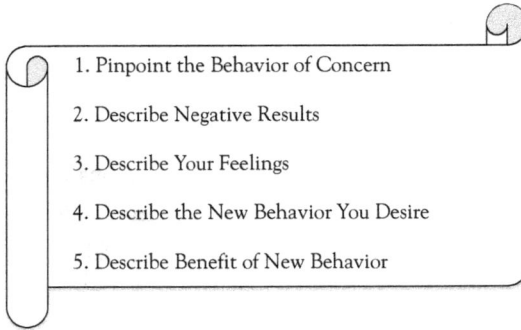

Figure 11.7 Correcting model

As you may recall from the chapters on communication, there is a formula for correcting behavior referred to as the Helpful Correcting Model. The leader described above used a similar process (Figure 11.7).

If you are having multiple conversations with an employee, it may be helpful to consider how you might use Positive Thinking and Celebrating Success as alternative behaviors you can use to influence behavior. For example, if your employee continues to submit projects late you may have more success using cause analysis to determine what is getting in the way of his submitting work on time. Recognizing work that is completed on time would also be important to encourage more of this behavior.

CHAPTER 12

Flexibility

Each of us has our own style of performing tasks and working with people. Much research on behavioral styles has been conducted to assist us understand how to work more effectively with others. If we want to influence and motivate individuals and work groups, understanding how they prefer to get their work done can assist you tailor your style to theirs.

For example, I know a talented and experienced individual who was recruited to work for a prestigious IT firm. He performs best when given assignments and left alone to accomplish them. He complained his manager reviewed his work every day and instructed him on next steps to take. Six months later he left to join a startup company. He was uncomfortable being micromanaged and left as a result.

Flexible leadership is critical for recruiting and retaining the talent needed to create and innovate. Therefore, it becomes incumbent on us to understand our style as well as the styles of our associates in order to lead individuals and work groups based on their styles for performing work. If we expect our associates to conform to our leadership style rather than adjusting our style for them we will continually experience low morale, turnover and minimal incentive on their part to share, to create, and to innovate. One style assessment used by a number of organizations is the DISC behavioral styles inventory.

D is Dominant. This style is goal oriented and measures success by achieving goals. May step on toes in the process. Tends to perform well in project management roles as an example. Let's getter done is their motto. Not very detail oriented.

I is Influence. This style is people oriented and performs well working with the public and individuals. Likes to please, loves parties and enjoys marketing and sales as an example. Never met a person they didn't like, you will hear. Not very detail oriented.

S is Steady. This style prefers having a game plan before starting work. Likes to plan and work the plan in other words. Is more detail minded and derives pleasure working on policy or being part of an operation's processes as an example. Will avoid conflict and resists changing the way work is done.

C is Conscientious. This style is highly detail oriented and works well performing tasks such as accounting or book editing. Do it right is their motto and you may have to follow up several times before you receive their work because they are checking it over again! This style does not like change and tends to avoid conflict.

How does all of this work for you or against you?

A colleague related how he had been recruited to join a small company. The firm consisted of two partners. The person interviewing him and making the decision possessed a similar behavioral style, Dominate. My friend, also style D, was happy and thrived until the other partner assumed responsibility for operations. He began experiencing stress and less enjoyment in his work. He soon left the organization. The other partner was a detailed oriented C! He later learned the firm experienced higher than desired turnover for years.

I coached a manager who was a high goal-oriented D. She could not comprehend why her staff did not cooperate with her. When staff completed the DISC inventory, she realized most staff used Steady and Conscientious styles. Bingo! They needed to know the process for performing their tasks and have the time to attend to details. The manager began assigning daily activities and tasks for each person, asking for their ideas when planning. Stress throughout the organization subsided and successful performance was achieved. The leader's new found flexibility improved operations because she responded to staff behavioral styles.

Now, should the manager have been Conscientious with a staff of Dominants her approach would change. She would achieve success by assigning her D's goals with the freedom to problem solve and plan how to achieve them. She would commit to her D's that their plans would not need to duplicate her method of work. Performance would soar to higher peaks.

Because any organization has a multitude of tasks, each style and combination of styles is necessary to be successful. Your role as a leader is to recognize the gifts each person offers and lead them in a manner that creates success for everyone. McDonald's has a saying when an operation is not performing well, "Get your aces in their places." When that happens, when you assign staff tasks they can succeed in performing using their preferred style of work, improvements happen.

What styles are evident in the following personalities? Circle the style you believe each uses. Keep in mind we all rely on several styles and your answer may include more than one option. At the bottom of the page are our best guesses!

Presidents:

1. Jimmy Carter: D I S C
2. Richard Nixon: D I S C
3. Bill Clinton: D I S C
4. Barack Obama: D I S C

Professions:

5. Accounting: D I S C
6. Nursing: D I S C
7. Sales: D I S C
8. Marketing: D I S C
9. Software Engineer: D I S C
10. Meeting Organizer: D I S C
11. Small Business Owner D I S C
     1=C, 2=D, 3=ID, 4=SD, 5=C, 6=SC, 7=DI, 8=S, 9=SC, 10=IS, 11=DI or SC

Plan of Action

After completing the survey identify what you want to change, what you should keep, and what should be discontinued.

Motivation Survey					
Behaviors	No 1	Poor 2	Adequate 3	Good 4	Very Good 5
Leader finds good in everyone					
We receive pats on the back					
We get together to celebrate when we accomplish our goals					
Leader catches us doing something good					
Leader tells us when we need to improve					
Leader gives four times more positive feedback than negative					
We have taken a behavior styles survey					
Our leader uses our preferred style					
We look forward to coming to work					

Figure 12.1 Motivation survey.

Start	Stop	Continue

Figure 12.2 Action plan

"We must cherish our imagination; our ability to dream; for the highest achievers since history began, have been the dreamers who, combined their perspiration and their aspiration to make their own unique contribution."

—Andrew Matthews, Being Happy!

An inventor lives asking the question, "What's missing in this picture?" and then answers it by inventing the missing piece that makes the picture whole.

—Michael E. Gerber, Awakening the Entrepreneur Within

"Creativity, by its very nature, often explores off of the beaten path and goes against the grain."

—John C. Maxwell, Thinking for a Change

CHAPTER 13

Proven Principles
of Innovation

We have explored leadership behaviors required for achieving success in a diverse culture. In this section, we will discuss innovation in its purest form. Until now, the examples convey incremental innovation resulting from improvement of an existing product or service. Innovation in its purest is creating a new product, service, or organization. This section will offer examples and ideas for creating new product or services incorporating principles of innovation. Practicing innovation principles, identifying demographic changes, defining and recruiting key skill sets, collaborative project leadership, encouraging play at work, and keeping secrets will lead to your success when innovating.

Thomas Edison considered all these factors when inventing the light bulb. He knew the changing demographic needs would be among wealthy home owners in the local area who would jump at the chance to have lighting with less risk of fire and no odor. He recruited persons with skills that could be used in the design and development not only of the light bulb but also the electric generator needed to produce electricity for his bulbs.

Edison led the design efforts challenging his recruits to develop alternative designs or solve design problems he was experiencing. He also assigned system design responsibilities to other team members. He normally worked with a project team of 12 or so specialists. Research has since shown that workgroups of 6 to 12 in size are optimum sizes for creative work groups. While being a workaholic, Edison was sensitive his staff needs of rest and relaxation and provided enough for them to remain loyal and creative. Edison was so concerned about keeping his designs confidential that he built a special facility outside of town. Everyone engaged in the project lived close by. He created a culture of creativity and innovation within his work environment.

Peter Drucker (2002), in his book, *Discipline of Innovation*, identified several principles to lead successful design and implementation efforts.

Analyze All Opportunity Sources

There is value in looking for as many opportunities as possible for new product or service offerings before settling on a single focus. Brainstorming and investigating alternative opportunities tends to create additional ideas leading to an even better final decision. The analysis considers return on investment (ROI) using criteria such as project costs, estimated design and production time, personnel competencies, and market receptivity required for the initiative.

Go Out, Look, Ask, and Listen

There can be a temptation to believe the engineering/marketing analysis serves needed investigation to begin design work. In a Wikipedia report, Ford's engineers created an innovative auto design that was certain to appeal to mass markets. The new model was named in honor of Henry Ford's son. After careful design and a well-planned marketing roll out in 1957, this new model was discontinued in 1959 reportedly due to its name and reliability problems. The car was the Edsel. Ford executives observed later, "The aim was right but the target moved."

Another automaker assigned a team of employees to live in California for 2 years. Their assignment was to drive a wide variety of vehicles and travel with California drivers to observe and define needs and preferences. Upon return to headquarters two years later, this team collaborated with corporate engineering to develop a new model car for the U.S. market. The car was the Toyota Camry.

The lesson is obvious. Ford marketing thought they understood the marketplace and designed accordingly. Toyota understood the importance of observing their target market, asking potential customers their ideas for improving existing vehicles, noting what they heard, and designing accordingly.

Simple and Focused

Keeping the final design simple and focused on market criteria is critical for building a quality product. Ford learned its lesson and took a different approach when designing their next new model offering. Before moving from design to build the concept was entered in an intramural design contest instigated by Lee Iacocca. The winning design was based on use of familiar but simple components and the name was based on research and comparison with public impressions. The new model became known as the Ford Mustang!

Aim to be Standard Setter

Whatever your new product is be certain it is of such a quality as to capture the market. It is not good enough to be first with a new idea. Thomas Edison created the first phonograph that caught the attention of the market. It was an immediate success; however, a competitor quickly offered another version that was easier to use and possessed higher sound quality. Edison was then faced with the decision to modify and catch up or refocus on other opportunities.

Apple's design of the ipod, ipad, and iphone all embrace the standard setter and simple and focused principles. The designs are simple but elegant, the parts are easily installed, and use of the products is simple to the point of nearly being intuitive. Much time and deliberation was involved in creating revolutionary products that challenge competitors to meet the high standards of quality in product design and ease of use.

A microchip manufacturer created a process for maintaining their position as standard setter in their marketplace. Each year, a multi-disciplinary team consisting of engineers, accountants, and marketing specialists visit customers such as IBM, Microsoft, and Nokia. The team identifies upcoming client initiatives and requirements. Many of these requirements are engineered into the next generation of microchips. However, when completing their design, the team leaves certain features out of the upcoming release to be included in the subsequent year's release. The strategy has kept the company one step ahead of its competitors and maintaining a standard for others to strive to meet.

Not Genius

We can all think of individuals such as Thomas Edison, Benjamin Franklin, Wright Brothers, Steve Jobs, Bill Gates, and many other truly gifted persons who pioneered innovations that have changed our lives and the world. However, even those individuals relied on teams of people with requisite skills and boatloads of common sense to create designs and plans for building new products and services. Even these visionaries gathered people around them and shared their ideas while engaging them in the creative side of new designs.

People with insight, knowledge, and talent come in all walks of life. We worked with a company who wanted to make major changes in the manner in which work was performed and technology was used in production. Executives were identifying people in their organization to participate on the innovation team. The consultant inquired about someone in the production area responsible for moving product around the work area. Executives explained the individual was not motivated and had limited knowledge of the operation. In talking with this individual, we learned he had never been asked to do anything other than his current duties but on his personal time served as Mayor of a neighboring community!

An executive with another client expressed delight when attending a design team meeting to hear an hourly employee explain why one idea could work but another could present difficulties for their clients! These design members were all geniuses when it came to their work and work processes.

Requires Hard, Focused, Purposeful Work

I doubt you would find an inventor who would say that his/her success came easily and the first idea was worth a million dollars. There are stories of how Silicon Valley

shifted from designing products to save the world to quickly designing software to be flipped for quick wealth.

Regardless of motivation, whether you are creating a website, designing a new application, creating a new product release or any other effort to innovate pulls the innovators into total engagement. Thomas Edison lived and worked in his facility even though his home was next door.

Steve Jobs along with any client I have served including myself will have inspirations day and night. Continuing to enhance the idea and bring it to life will have you leaping out of bed late at night to record your next great idea or work more on your design. Expect to spend all hours of your day researching and developing your product launch plan and systems to support the idea you have successfully introduced to the market.

Talent

Determining required talent is part intuition and part deliberation once the focus on new organization, product, or service has been agreed upon. It is not at all unusual for talent requirements to change as the innovation project is underway. We were asked to recruit electrical engineers for a company producing and marketing fish finding equipment. Our client completed a discovery process using focus groups with fishing professionals and hobbyists. The focus group data, aligned with the principle Going Out, Looking, Asking, and Listening, indicated a need to completely innovate their fish finding products to remain competitive in their market. It became clear to our client that not only electrical engineers but also mechanical engineers would be required for a complete reengineering of their product lines.

CHAPTER 14

Organizing and Managing Innovation

Project Structure

Key elements include establishing a project structure, developing a project plan and budget, recruiting resources, project training of project teams and facilitating project team meetings, and communication between project members and the community.

The project structure includes a Steering Committee made up of key representatives of your organization, along with key stakeholders and customers. This committee meets monthly to provide guidance and remove barriers for the project teams.

The second element of the project structure consists of project teams for each new innovation. These teams meet weekly, review and update project plans, solve problems, and agree on plans for the following week. They attend monthly Steering Committee meetings to report on progress and share information.

The third element of the project structure includes project Subject Matter Experts such as customers, technical specialists, research personnel, and others who provide research, education, information, and council to accommodate project design and implementation plans. The project manager facilitates decision making events, attends and updates project status at steering committee meetings, facilitates project team meetings, and tracks project tasks and financial activities.

Project management utilizes many of the leadership behaviors discussed previously and will be referenced as we discuss key elements of

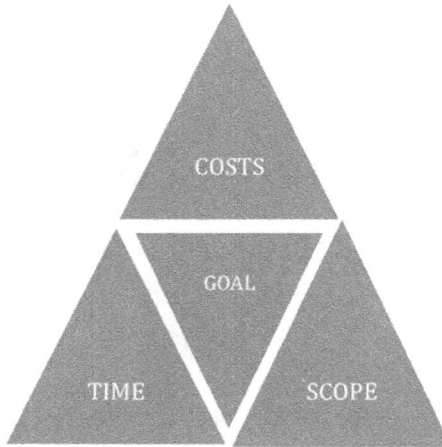

Figure 14.1 Project scope

leading innovation design or redesign initiatives. The beginning involves defining project goals in measurable terms. For example, the innovation goal of XYZ company is to design a fish finding system for up to minute tracking of fish by December 15, 2016.

Defining the goal serves to determine estimates for elapsed time for project completion, project scope regarding time, personnel, material supplies (computers, manuals, networking equipment, and so on), resources (consultants, access to data, and so on), and finally cost estimates based on time and scope deliberations (Figure 14.1).

Project Management Roadmap

There are four key elements or steps involved in leading an innovation project through to successful completion. Figure 14.2 illustrates each step including **Initiate, Plan, Implement**, and **Close** out the project.

Project Roles

For a project of any sort to be successful, there are several roles to be filled during the project lifecycle. Those roles include:

Sponsor: Provides authorization and funding for the project. Additionally provides information for project goals and objectives and makes final decision on project plans and execution.

Customer: Persons receiving program services. Provide project requirements, goals and objectives, and communicates with the project manager and team leader during the project and may attend team meetings.

Stakeholders: Anyone affected by the project. May not receive the services of the project but have a stake in the project such as resource providers, community members and suppliers. They may attend team meetings and benchmark updates.

Project manager: Manages the project and team members, communicates regularly with the sponsor, customers, and designated stakeholders on progress, and is accountable for bringing the project in on time and within budget.

Team leader: May be the project manager or someone who manages parts of the project and is accountable for communicating with and motivating team members, ensuring other project groups are communicated with, and delivering his/her part of the project in on time and within budget.

Team members: Members are specialists who possess critical knowledge and skills required for the project.

Resource manager: Provides resources for the project such as information technology, materials, technical knowledge, and facilities.

Administrative support: Provides administrative support for scheduling, updating project data, reporting plans, and coordinating team member activities.

Initiate	Plan	Implement	Close
Sponsors & project manager	Sponsors, project manager, team & stakeholders	Sponsors, project manager, team & stakeholders	Sponsors, project manager & team
Specify problem or opportunity	Develop plan goals, business case & schedule. Confirm costs and scope.	Monitor project progress & make changes	Formally close out the project
Determine project costs & benefits	Identify tasks, resources, responsibilities & target dates. Assign authority.	Communicate progress & changes regularly & frequently to customers & stakeholders	Evaluate project success & challenges & document changes in processes for next project
Obtain approval & recruit project team	Monitor/anticipate risks	Respond to changes & keep sponsors informed	Celebrate!!!

Figure 14.2 Project roles and tasks

Business Case

The business case is designed in the *Initiate Phase* and is used to request project funding and/or organizational support for your initiative. The process is similar to many fund application processes used by grantees and has been helpful to others when thinking through the key elements of the innovation to be attempted.

Plan The Plan

The purpose of **Project Planning** (Figure 14.3) is to:

A. Develop measurable goals and objectives for the project.
B. Identify stakeholders who will be affected by the project and develop collaboration between the project team and stakeholders.
C. Determine the cost and scope of the project.
D. Identify tasks, expertise needed, responsibilities, authority, target dates and timelines.
E. Anticipate risk.
F. Secure support and approvals and develop a budget.

Project: Software Implementation	
Project Sponsors	Sue Williams, Program Director
Priority (High, Medium, Low)	Medium
Success Measures	#Staff complaints, #reports completed on time, Hrs. downtime
Tangible Deliverables	PCs, wireless equipment, operating and user software
Intangible Deliverables	Staff communication, staff training
Costs	Cost Estimate: $25,000.00
Benefits	Benefits: Reduced complaints, increased number of reports completed on time.
Alternatives for addressing the issue faster, at less cost, more efficiently	Adding wireless with current hardware not feasible, several vendors evaluated and this was most cost effective considering location of this vendor.
Risks	Technology changes creating added costs, inflation adding costs, shipment delays.
Sustainability	Funds needed for two phases, funds available for first phase only
Next Steps	Authorize vendor to present to staff.
Sponsor's Approval	

Figure 14.3 Project plan

Project Goals

The purpose of the project goal is to provide clear focus for the project. Project objectives are used to determine project resources and budget.

Goal statements include required action, costs, and timeline for the project.

Examples:

1. Develop three storybooks for ages 3 to 5 by March 30, 2009, within the budget of $28,000.
2. Conduct energy audit of 20 county buildings to identify short- and long-term initiatives for increasing energy efficiency and reducing costs by April 15, 2017.

   Once the goals are established, you are in position to determine how feasible your initiative may be. Considerations include project scope, deliverables, resources, and potential constraints. A worksheet for determining your project's feasibility is illustrated in Figure 14.4.

Project Goal:	Develop 3 storybooks for ages 3–5 by March 30, 2009 within a budget of $28,000.
Scope/Deliverables	
Financial Program Operations Technology Strategic Plan Quality	Salary and materials estimated to be $28,000. Books, materials, furnishings, equipment Wireless computer system, Microsoft operating systems, video systems The project is one of 10 initiatives of our nonprofit Must appeal to community, be fun and hands-on.
Resources	
Funds People Materials & Equipment Facilities	$10,000 from state funds, $15,000 from county funds, $3,000 from "Give Kids a Chance" 5k race Parents, learning specialists from XYZ University, nonprofit project manager. 3 computers using software designed for learning projects. Our office and local library will serve for collaboratives.
Constraints	
Physical/Technical Legal/Policies Customer Needs	Risk of computer software being delayed State budget could cause delays Fast growing population along with stagnant funding for early childhood development could limit distribution to target population.

Figure 14.4 Feasibility worksheet

The Work Plan

Work Breakdown Structure

A key element of the plan is organizing tasks for scheduling your work and fine-tuning the budget. Mind mapping is a proven tool for effectively and efficiently identifying and categorizing tasks. The goal is stated in the circle and tasks to accomplish the goal are brainstormed and listed on branches (Figure 14.5).

After organizing tasks, the resources and budget can be determined. The worksheet shown in Figure 14.6 is a tool for determining a budget for your project.

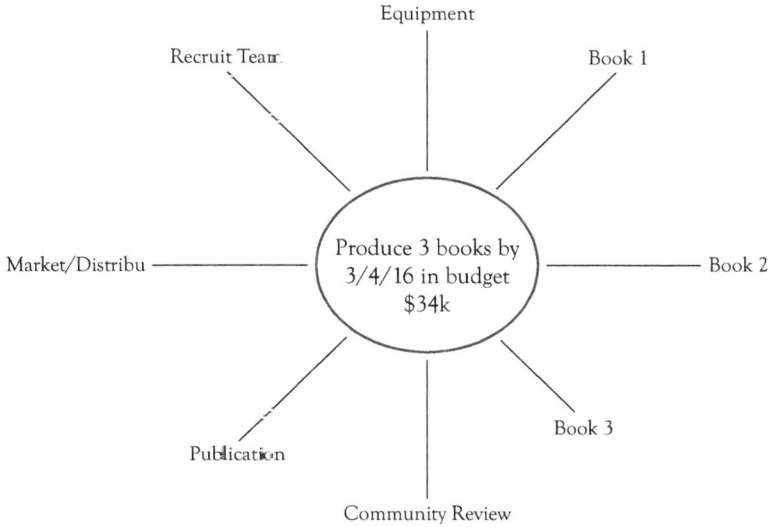

Figure 14.5 Work breakdown structure

Project Budget				
Task	**Resources**	**Quantity**	**Cost**	**Total**
Recruit team	XYZ Early Childhood specialists & Early Childhood Centers	3 specialists 4 center leaders		$8,500
Pour concrete pad	Southern Concrete	1,500 sq. yd.	12,000	12,000
Install stick built walls	SM Construction	5 men × 15 d	3,000 × 15	$45,000
Install roof trusses	TRC Roofing	20 Trusses 2 men × 2 d	250 1,000 × 2	$5,000 $2,000
Exterior siding	Hardwood Lumber Co. Top Notch Operations	2,000 ft. 2 men × 9 days	3,000 1,000 × 9	$3,000 $9,000
Roof decking	Jennings Top Notch Ops	1,500 sq. ft. 2 men × 2 d	1,500 1,000 × 2	$1,500 $2,000
Roof shingles	Jennings Top Notch Ops	1,500 sq. ft. 2 men × 4 d	$3,000 1,000 × 4	$3,000 $4,000
Interior wall finishing	Hardwood Top Notch Ops	125 sheets 4 men × 5 d	$7 2,000 × 5	$875 $10,000
Concrete floor staining	Top Notch	2,000 sq. ft.	$5 × 2,000	$10,000

Figure 14.6 Budget example

Gantt Charts and Action Plans

Gantt Charts were developed to depict the project plan and provide a means for monitoring and communicating progress by project milestones (Figure 14.7). Smaller projects may use an Action Planning format instead for monitoring progress and problem solving (Figure 14.8).

Approval Process

1. To avoid problems, it is advisable to obtain approval for moving ahead at each stage of the project.
2. Once your plan is developed, the project should be approved with a signature by the project sponsor.

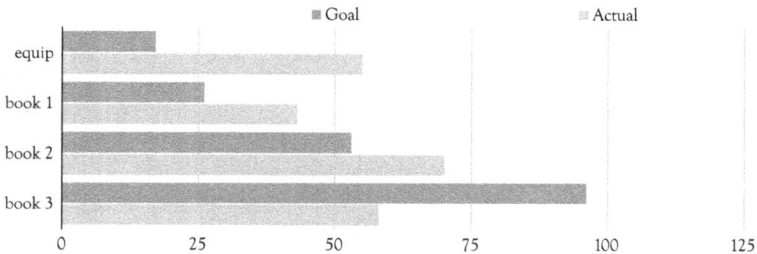

Figure 14.7 Gantt chart

Action Plan			
What	**Who**	**When**	**Actual**

Figure 14.8 Action plan

3. The team or project sponsor can use the action planning form described earlier, a Gantt chart, or other agreed upon document for obtaining needed review and approvals at each stage or milestone of your project.

Communicate and Evaluate

Project teams will have a schedule for communicating progress and obtaining approval for changes and to proceed to next milestone.

Typically, a weekly or biweekly meeting will be scheduled with the project sponsor and key stakeholders for information sharing and decision making on the project.

In those meetings, the project team will review their Gantt Chart or Action Plan worksheet and solicit input and support from sponsor and stakeholders.

Those meetings should begin with the project plan review meeting in which final approval for the plan is obtained, processes for purchasing are agreed upon, and a meeting schedule is determined.

CHAPTER 15

Creative and Confidential

A young man went to his father to announce he wanted to get married. His father asked who the girl was. His son told him it was Mary Lou, a girl from the neighborhood. His father sadly said, "I'm sorry son but the girl you wish to marry is your sister. Please don't tell your mother."

The son brought more names to his father only to be frustrated with the same response! So . . . the son decided to tell his mother. Mom, he said, "I want to get married but dad said the girls are all my sisters." His mother smiled and said, "don't worry, you can marry any one of those girls. You're not his son!"

Whether at home or work, maintaining secrets requires attention to the human element of confidentiality and ever more to technical security.

Confidentiality

Employees tend to protect the organization for whom they work. However, no matter how loyal and careful the management and workforce may be accidents can happen. Several considerations to prevent "loose lips" include the following:

Assemble your team and explain the importance of the project to their company's success.

1. Let them know the consequences to our company should the information get into the public domain or be obtained by a competitor.
2. Provide an incentive for the team to maintain confidences such as awarding stock, providing a percentage of new product revenue for a specified time or other rewards of value to the team. Furthermore, let them know the consequences they will experience should project information be divulged.

3. Tell the team how long information must be confidential. Remind them that a good practice when communicating electronically is to ask if the information should be secure. If the answer is yes, then encrypt or use another mean for communicating with other team members.

4. Give team members the opportunity to opt out of the project if they think they would be unable to keep secrets.

5. Some organizations will use non-disclosure agreements to be reviewed and signed by each team member. The document might include provisions discussed in this section.

A completely different approach to protecting secrets is employed by a variety of technology driven companies such as Apple. The team is organized into sub teams, that is, separate work cells. Each cell has a portion of the product to develop and the cells do not communicate with one another. As a result, no one can fully describe the product until its release. Reports indicate this approach was used successfully with iPhone development.

There is no foolproof way to prevent mistakes or deliberate mischief when working with people. The suggestions above only serve to minimize the chance for leaks. For that reason, it is helpful to have a plan B should information be leaked. For example, Lee Iacocca wanted to compete with GM's Camero. Ford had experienced a disaster when creating the Edsel so Iacocca chose to do everything differently when creating his vision. During the design phase, the public and competitors were lead to believe the Edsel would serve as the model for the new car. The revised Edsel took America by storm, it was a Mustang!

Technology Challenges

According to the publication, *High Tech Highway,* the greatest threat to breach of confidentiality, is the growth of personal devices within the workplace.

Applications for preventing a breach or theft include:

1. Mobile Device Management (MDM) solutions enable a company to lock or wipe devices if lost or stolen. As important as it is to secure company devices, it is as important to secure personal devices that

can be left around or misplaced creating opportunities for information leaks and security breaches. This point should be clearly communicated to all members in the workforce.

2. Mobile Application Management (MAM) secures company technology by restricting access to certain data or systems based on defined criteria such as an employee's position, pay level, reporting level or duties in the company.

3. According to Ryan Sobel in his article, *Keeping Company Secrets a Secret with Geo Fencing* reports that Geo Fencing is a system that can develop barriers in an office restricting or disabling mobile devices from sending photographs, texting or videos outside the perimeter.

Play Purposefully

"There is good evidence that if you allow employees to engage in something they want to do, (which) is playful, there are better outcomes in terms of productivity and motivation."

—Dr. Stuart Brown,
Founder of the National Institute for Play

"I think there are some enlightened companies that are beginning to get this, especially companies in research and development and design," said Dr. Stuart Brown, founder of the National Institute for Play.

Brown offers play consulting for tech and non-tech companies alike, including Whole Foods. The reason: Not only does having a playful atmosphere attract young talent, but experts say play at work can boost creativity and productivity in people of all ages.

Play can also lower your stress levels, boost your optimism, and increase your motivation to move up in a company and improve concentration and perseverance. There's some evidence from animal studies that engaging in play opens up new neural connections in the brain, leading to greater creativity, he added.

All sorts of creative new connections are made when you're playing that otherwise would never be made.

Playing also engages the creative side of your brain. When you're fully engaged in play, you lose some of your psychological barriers and stop censoring or editing your thoughts. This allows creative ideas to flow more freely.

"It's not just the activity of playing that encourages creativity. When companies promote play, it engenders a more lighthearted atmosphere."

We need to trust to play and to be creative. The ping-pong table in the office reminds people they work in a permissive and playful environment. Putting a bunch of action figures or tactile puzzles in the center of a conference room table can automatically lighten the mood of the meetings.

You can look at the people standing in line to buy lunch and make up stories about their lives.

"Begin to have a sense of richness from your own internal thought process", Stuart Brown said. Take mini-breaks, and think back to a time when you were more carefree, even to childhood; and visualize yourself doing something that was completely enjoyable. You may realize that something is missing from your life and re-introduce it. If you loved competitive sports, maybe you'd join a tennis league. If you loved photography, maybe you can bring your camera to work and take creative breaks.

"Work hard to bring that playful spirit into the office on Monday morning."

Keep It Creative

Over the years whether redesigning corporations, setting up team-based operations, facilitating problem solving sessions, resolving conflicts and creating trust, conducting focus groups, and/or coaching leaders, I have discovered several proven steps that unleash the creativity you seek.

1. Become a facilitator.

Being a facilitator means first giving up the need to have the answer. Your job is not to lead others to your conclusion, instead it is to lead your group to a solution, product, service, or new organization that solves the challenge and excites the group. Second, your role is to ask questions that do not lead to an obvious conclusion. Instead questions should be open and look at the challenge in different ways to provide the best conclusion. For example, Howard Schultz, CEO of Starbucks, originally pursued the concept of replicating the Italian coffee shop. His question was, "How can I recreate the Italian espresso bar in the United States?" He later changed his perspective and instead asked, "How can I create a comfortable, relaxing environment to enjoy great coffee?" A different question creates a different set of solutions!

Asking the question one way, then altering the question for more ideas can be helpful in avoiding the trap of asking the wrong question. For example, when working with an engineering group the first question was, "How do we solve the parking problem on campus?" After brainstorming for a while, the question was changed to, What do commuting students face and what would they suggest?, then, What would faculty suggest? and finally, "What wild and crazy ideas do you have?" While some ideas were similar the new questions always created more ideas than before.

Your role as a facilitator is to ask the questions, record answers as expressed by members of your group, and refrain from offering solutions yourself. You will find they will suggest solutions similar to your idea and more that can create a more comprehensive solution. Group members typically get off track and begin having discussions. Refocus them on brainstorming by reminding them of the question being addressed.

2. *Create play time.*

When adults play, minds wander and the subconscious is given opportunity to go to work. This is why time off from work is necessary for creativity to bloom. I imagine you have been stumped when attempting to solve a problem only to find the answer while taking a walk or engaging in an activity totally unrelated to your work situation. I find that when unable to think through a problem, taking a run usually relaxes my mind permitting my subconscious to work overtime leading to resolution of problems or creation of a new idea. Harry Truman was known to leave Washington DC to return to his farm when being challenged with issues in congress. After cutting a cord of wood or plowing the back 40, Truman would return to DC refreshed and ready to tackle challenges thrown at him.

When working with a client I always have tennis balls, hula hoops, and a rope available to provide play time and help people think out of the box. Recently, I helped a small business think through ways to improve revenue and reduce costs. The owners and staff were given an exercise to go through a hula hoop together. My goal was to open their minds to new ways to collaborate and make decisions. The owners initiated regular communication and problem solving meetings with staff and their business began improving.

When you think about offering play exercises for your staff consider the following guidelines:

- 10 minute exercises create awareness.
- 10 to 30 minute exercises begin skill development
- 2 to 3 hour exercises begin changing attitudes.

The most effective exercises include opportunity for participants to see, hear, and touch during their time together. Having free time at work to play games, relax, and share ideas is also valuable for enhancing creativity at work. Keep children's play toys and games around to encourage discussion and new ideas.

3. *Encourage out of box ideas.*

Creative leaders are always on the lookout for great ideas. You can do this by practicing mindfulness, which involves intentionally noticing things and letting your mind relax and focus. Research has shown we lose our creativity as we allow ourselves to work longer hours and sleep less. Failing to restore our bodies and minds with sufficient sleep leads to greater tension, more frustration and higher levels of anxiety. To set the climate for out of the box thinking, it is incumbent on any leader to get between 7 and 10 hours of sleep each night and encourage everyone in their workforce to do the same. Decision-making ability is depleted when we are tired. Bill Clinton stated every mistake he made was when he was tired. We are much more effective and able to create when our energy is not depleted. For that reason, any leader who encourages full sleep at night and naps at work will renew energy, mental alertness and creative thinking on the part of themselves and their associates.

Do not let accidents discourage or distract you. Instead approach them as learning opportunities that can lead to new ideas. Inventions such as Posted Notes and The Slinky were created because someone asked why their initiative did not work and how their unintended result could benefit in another way.

4. *Develop concepts from list of "out of the box" ideas.*

   Two time-tested methods exist for making sense out of a long list of ideas in order to develop a new concept. Both methods are based on high level participation and consensus decisions.

   A. *The 80/20 Rule* is based on scientific study that concludes eighty percent of anything is caused or cured by twenty percent of something. According to Wikipedia, "The Pareto principle (also known as the 80–20 rule, the law of the vital few, and the principle of factor sparsity)[1] states that, for many events, roughly 80% of the effects come from 20% of the causes.[2] Management consultant Joseph M. Juran suggested the principle and named it after Italian economist Vilfredo Pareto, who, while at the University of Lausanne in 1896, published his first paper "Cours d'économie politique." Essentially, Pareto showed that approximately 80% of the land in Italy was owned by 20% of the population; Pareto developed the principle by observing that 20% of the peapods in his garden contained 80% of the peas.[3] It is a common rule of thumb in business; e.g., "80% of your sales come from 20% of your clients." Mathematically, the 80–20 rule is roughly followed by a power law distribution (also known as a Pareto distribution) for a particular set of parameters, and many natural phenomena have been shown empirically to exhibit such a distribution.[4]

McDonalds Corporation asked me to work with their Owner Operator market team in Colorado. This group of 20 to 30 restaurants was experiencing challenges maintaining inventory, long drive through times and order accuracy well below standard. We spent a morning clarifying the problem (ask the right questions) after which we brainstormed causes to the problems. Using the 80/20 rule, the operators voted on the six out of thirty issues causing most of the problems. The six causes were then listed on the wall, and a list of solutions were brainstormed for each cause. Twenty percent of the solutions were selected and put into an action plan for monthly review. This market team set new records for reduced drive through time and increased order accuracy. Additionally, they began sharing inventory so that no restaurant would run out of food or supplies.

a. B. Affinity diagram
b. From Wikipedia, the free encyclopedia
c. Affinity wall diagram
d. "The affinity diagram is a business tool used to organize ideas and data. It is one of the Seven Management and Planning Tools. People have been grouping data into groups based on natural relationships for thousands of years; however, the term affinity diagram was devised by Jiro Kawakita in the 1960s[1] and is sometimes referred to as the KJ Method.
e. The tool is commonly used within project management and allows large numbers of ideas stemming from brainstorming[2] to be sorted into groups, based on their natural relationships, for review and analysis.[3] It is also frequently used in contextual inquiry as a way to organize notes and insights from field interviews. It can also be used for organizing other freeform comments, such as open-ended survey responses, support call logs, or other qualitative data.
f. Process
g. The affinity diagram organizes ideas with following steps:
5. Record each idea on cards or notes.
6. Look for ideas that seem to be related.
7. Sort cards into groups until all cards have been used.
   Once the cards have been sorted into groups the team may sort large clusters into subgroups for easier management and analysis.[4] Once completed, the affinity diagram may be used to create a cause and effect diagram.[5]
   In many cases, the best results tend to be achieved when the activity is completed by a cross-functional team, including key stakeholders. The process requires becoming deeply immersed in the data, which has benefits beyond the tangible deliverables."

The Eastern Band of Cherokee Indians requested assistance with merging two operations into a single program. The first step was to clarify their strategy, then analyze work processes and technology after which we analyzed human resource systems to insure everything would work well together. Particularly when assessing Human Resource systems we found affinity diagrams to be quite helpful. We were organized into a cross functional design team and using cards to list issues and sort through them kept deliberations moving forward and eliminated potential conflicts between the merging groups.

8. Develop a project plan

   Create a prototype. Ford engineers used clay to design automobile prototypes, another organization used drawings to picture the type of organization being envisioned, others may use picture collages, and others may use child toys or legos to create the visuals for a new concept. Using any of these tools serve to bring clarity to your project while creating excitement and ownership on the part of the project team and stakeholders.

   After gaining clarity, it is time to use your project management tools discussed earlier with decision trees and action planning to organize tasks and initiate development of your exciting concept.

Case Studies

CULTURE OF INNOVATION
(McDonald's Corporation)

We have discussed the importance of engaging in the behaviors discussed in this book with examples to provide insight. To conclude our discussions, I am providing you a case study to illustrate how using all the behaviors has transformed an operation into the most competitive and dominant enterprise in their marketplace.

Situation:

This client constructed restaurants throughout the eastern seaboard of the United States. Two units were responsible for all production. One unit (Real Estate) had the responsibility for identifying suitable sites and purchasing land. The second unit (Construction) was responsible for design and build of restaurants on the sites. Each team consists of 5 to 10 members. Each team employed a director-level manager for leadership and guidance to their teams. Together the teams had constructed no more than seven units in a year.

Conflicts caused by rivalry and blaming were well known regarding these two groups. It was described to me as each unit throwing grenades over the wall into the other unit's workplace. The managers did not communicate well with each other or with their units. Unit members were verbally chastised in public when things went wrong and things frequently went wrong! The groups blamed each other for problems and within each group members were singled out for blame, not infrequently by other unit members. As a result, members avoided coming to the office and came prepared to defend themselves when they had to meet. The managers gave work assignments to each person individually and separate from the others.

The region updated its strategy for the year and agreed on a highly aggressive goal for restaurant construction. In addition, these two units were tasked with creating a new restaurant model. The units were challenged to innovate the manner in which they performed their duties and to create a model for constructing a totally new restaurant for the region. Shortly after the strategy session, one of the unit managers was transferred to an overseas assignment.

New Beginning

I suggested to the regional executive vice president (EVP) a different approach be taken with these units. Rather than hiring a new manager, use the remaining manager as project leader for both units and provide time for them to reorganize around their new strategy. He agreed and added that should these units build 30 restaurants within the strategy period he would send every member to Hawaii for a week's vacation.

Behaviors: Aligning Vision and Strategy, Planning and Organizing With Strategy, Linking Customers with Staff, and Regular Meeting Schedules.

We then held an intensive two-day retreat in which every member of these two units along with their manager participated in creating a new vision, mission, and principles for the whole group based on their challenge from the regional strategy. They then identified measures for production, costs, sales, and customer count along with a timeframe for restaurant construction. They were taught how to analyze their work processes, and after visualizing the work of each unit, they recognized the similarity of each groups' work and the problems each experienced. They began innovating the manner in which they would perform their work, divide up work, and work together. They practiced using a problem solving model and began resolving causes of their conflicts. Finally, when considering customer requirements they realized the best way to satisfy their markets would be to organize into two units containing both real estate and construction personnel, that is, cross-functional work teams, and agreed for Team A to work one side of the Potomac and Team B the other side. Each team then chose a team leader for their team and agreed to report progress to the manager together rather than individually. Each team agreed on a weekly meeting schedule coordinated with the other team and a monthly meeting for the whole group.

Behaviors: Listening Before Speaking, Building Trust, and Modeling Ethical Behavior

As each team began meeting, the manager would attend but would not speak unless asked a question directly. Many times he would refer the question to the team leader. He made it clear to the team that the team leader should lead the meeting. To build trust among the members, any problem brought up in the meeting was treated as an opportunity to solve the problem and learn from the experience. A team member having difficulty was celebrated for raising the issue and members began offering ideas and personal assistance. To encourage ethical behavior, each group established a code of conduct for their group and codes were reviewed each week at the start of the meeting.

Behaviors: Drive out Fear, Facilitate, Encourage New Ideas, and Delegate.

As the teams were formed and began functioning, anxiety and fear of blaming still existed. To reduce the anxiety, the manager delegated to his team leaders the responsibility for starting the meetings with something fun like a guessing game, or exercise using tennis balls. In addition, he would tell them of his failures when doing similar work to let them know they have company and understanding. Team leaders began describing their "humanness" also. Combined with using problem solving to address roadblocks on projects these tactics began not only eliminating fear within the groups but also began creating innovative ideas that were incorporated into the way work was performed. Members began opening up and risking as a result of experiencing not only the ability to problem solve work issues but having the responsibility for making changes delegated to them.

Facilitation and delegation became a way of life for the team leaders and manager. For example, when problem solving, the leader used round robin or freewheeling combined with open-ended questions to determine along with team members the causes of project delays or cost overruns. Open questions were used to determine solutions. Members were asked to choose the actions they should take and determine timelines for getting tasks completed. These behavioral changes resulted in creation of many new ideas that became part of a new work system and restaurant model.

Behaviors: Celebrating Improvement and Goal Attainment, Positive Thinking, Calm Correcting, and Flexible Styles.

In weekly meetings, each team took time for others on the team to recognize each other for achievements or help received. If the teams met weekly goals, they would go to lunch together. In their monthly meeting, the summary scorecard was reviewed reflecting the achievements of both teams together. The review was in the office hallway where other staff and management could see and hear. Goal achievements were recognized with cheers and hand clapping before going to lunch together. Each month the group was reminded of how close they were coming to their trip to Hawaii.

Flexibility when working with each team became an important consideration. Some team members had much experience and needed very little coaching whereas others had limited experience and needed much more coaching and mentoring. As the teams began maturing, the manager and team leaders realized they could delegate much more than in the past and with some experimentation began finding how much authority and decision making the teams could be assigned. For example, the teams were not able to negotiate with architects or contractors in the beginning. However, after contractors began attending team meetings, it was clear the team had developed to the point they were able to negotiate fairly with their contractors and architects. One team member even began helping contractors improve their work processes to get restaurants built quicker and more efficiently.

Another example illustrates how human resource systems may interfere with attempts to be creative and innovate. The group manager wanted new hire orientation to be conducted by the team. He could not understand why the teams would not take time to train new team members and show them the ropes. It was only after a team member explained that if he took the requisite time to orient someone he would not be working on his project. He would have a poor performance review and could lose his year-end bonus. Both the pay and performance review systems were rewarding individual contributions that discouraged group collaboration and ability to innovate. Later that year, the performance review and bonus systems were changed to encourage time for orientation and collaboration. The teams began new hire orientation and moved forward collaborating and implementing ideas for meeting their goals.

From time to time, a team member would experience personal problems. In those situations, the manager would invite the person to his office for calm problem solving. Very rarely was there a need for progressive discipline in this new environment.

Regarding positive thinking, a manager explained to me how negative the environment used to be. Their policies described infractions or violations leading to termination. The leadership team realized that newly hired personnel were being confronted with termination before even being on the job a week. They discarded the policies and instituted a one-page list of positive behaviors expected of everyone.

Outcome:

By creating a total environment dedicated to collaboration, creation, and innovation, leaders created a totally new culture. The organization became highly competitive in its marketplace. One competitor left the market altogether as over 30 new restaurants were built and all restaurants in the system became highly efficient and customer focused. Additionally, new revenue was generated that year and the 20 members of the two project teams thoroughly enjoyed time with their families in Hawaii!

CULTURE OF INNOVATION
(EBCI Travel and Tourism)

More recently, a travel and tourism client went through a similar initiative. The initiatives' goal was to create greater capacity to produce within the operation. Leaders were trained and coached, and the organization was organized in collaborative work groups. Managers began facilitating rather than dictating and delegating decisions and responsibilities. In this new culture of collaboration and innovation, work groups created more new events faster than before, doubling the number and type of events over the same period the previous year. The quality of events improved and the number of people attending events increased.

The organization performed at this level with fewer people than the year before. Another consulting firm was contracted to merge several programs including my client. These consultants told my client's personnel who they would be working for, assigned the group a strategy designed by the consultants, and redefined individual responsibilities. Additionally, the leader was replaced with a more traditional manager. Employees reverted to individual work silos. Productivity and performance declined to prior levels. Initiatives to create new events or improve the way work was performed ceased.

CREATING NEW PRODUCTS AND SERVICES
(Clemson University)

Peter Drucker noted several factors to consider when collaborating to create a new organization, product, or service. He observed the most reliable of innovation opportunities have to do with changing demographics such as population numbers, age, education, occupation, and geographic location.

An example he cites is Japan's venture into robotics. Over 10 years ago executives in Japan realized the number of people working in production would be diminishing worldwide within the foreseeable future. The result was development of a national strategy to create robots to address the anticipated labor shortage. Recently, Google began buying robotics companies to close the lead Japan has gained in the quickly expanding robotic market.

I was invited to present to a Travel and Tourism business class at Clemson University. We discussed the issues in new business start-ups after which they were organized into two business groups. Changing demographics were reviewed with each group after which they were assigned the task of creating a product or service to address either one or a combination of changing population numbers, age range, education levels, occupation, and geographic location. At the end of 30 minutes, each team reported out. One business team identified their market needs as parents coming to campus. They designed an app to inform parents of available parking when arriving on campus for football games and other events. The other business team identified their market to be retired persons living in the state of Florida. They developed a series of unique services for these individuals.

These students had begun the innovation process. After their collaboration to create concepts they were prepared to focus on the principles of "Analyze all Opportunities" along with "Go Out, Look, Ask and Listen."

SOLVING A PARKING PROBLEM ON CAMPUS
(Western Carolina University)

Recently, I spoke to an engineering class at Western Carolina University. I told them about my son who is a mechanical engineering student in

Georgia. He asked me to attend the school's Pumpkin Chunking event. His class had been challenged to design and build catapults that could chunk a pumpkin across the school lawn. The best catapult won an award. I came to the big day only to see my son very discouraged. He explained that his team's device could not win because of its design. Two members of their team insisted on their design idea and the team went along with them (group think). Sure enough, when the time came for the team to chunk its pumpkin, the catapult failed. Several tense minutes passed as the team frantically made adjustments and finally chunked their pumpkin a short distance.

In class we discussed the importance of collaboration and consensus building when innovating to avoid the problems experienced by our pumpkin chunking team. The 35 mechanical engineering students were taught the concepts of brainstorming. We reviewed the three types: free-wheeling to stimulate out of the box and random ideas, round robin to ensure quiet people and anyone else not yet participating have a chance to be heard, and slip method for situations in which tension exists or communication is just not happening within the group. We then reviewed key guidelines including "go for quantity," "no discussion," and "build on ideas."

The class was then challenged to solve the parking problem on campus. Using Free Wheeling and Round Robin, the students created over 25 ideas, some quite unique and creative. Using Round Robin, the group then voted to select one item having the most potential for solving the problem. Not surprising, their solution was a parking garage. Innovation occurred when the class built on the idea. The garage changed to an underground garage (avoids interfering with views of the surrounding mountains and provides energy efficient heating). They suggested graveled satellite parking areas to handle overflow. Segway devices were considered a green alternative to other forms of transportation and would be available in the garage for students traveling across campus. Everyone in class voted and reached consensus on their final design. We reviewed how their ideas could be applied to a decision tree for fully scoping out the project and how an action plan could serve as a tool for successful project implementation.

In summary, establishing a culture of collaboration and creativity, combined with tools for managing and implementing new concepts, can renew your organization and move it forward in existing as well as new markets. Complete the survey below to determine what you can stop, start, and continue doing to become sustainable in competitive in your markets.

Figure 1

Culture Survey

Score the behaviors listed below. For all staff and management.

Behavior	Not at all 1	Infrequently 2	Some times 3	Frequently 4	Always 5
Develops Vision & Strategy with Staff					
Plans & Organizes Work with Staff					
Links Customers with Staff					
Builds Trust					
Meets Regularly with Staff					
Models Ethical Behavior					
Drives Away Fear					
Listens Before Speaking					
Facilitates to Solve Problems with Staff					
Encourages New Ideas					
Delegates					
Celebrates Improvements & Goal Attainment					
Thinks Positively					
Calmly Corrects					
Flexible with Staff					
Follow Innovation Principles					
Use Project Management Tools					
Have Policies for Confidentiality					
Encourage Play					

References

Dittman, M. June, 2005. "Generational Differences at Work." *American Psychological Association Monitor* 36, no. 6, p. 54.

Page, S. November 13, 2015. "Ben Bernanke: More Execs Should Have Gone to Jail for Causing Great Recession." *USA Today*.

Heath, C., and D. Heath. 2013. "The Four Villains of Decision Making." In *Decisive,* eds. C. Heath, and D. Heath. New York, NY: Crown Business, pp. 9–29.

Daniels, A. 2000. "The ABCs of Performance Management." In *Bringing Out the Best in People*, ed. A. Daniels. New York, NY: McGraw-Hill, pp. 34–52.

Drucker, P. August 2002. "The Discipline of Innovation. 1985." *Harvard Business Review* 80, no. 8, pp. 95–100.

Wikipedia. "Innovation Ford Mustang."

Wikipedia. "Innovation Edsel."

Brown, S. September 15, 2012. "Work Hard, Play Harder: Fun at Work Boosts Creativity, Productivity." *Fox News Health*.

Wikipedia. "Affinity Diagrams."

Index

OTHER TITLES IN THE HUMAN RESOURCE MANAGEMENT AND ORGANIZATIONAL BEHAVIOR COLLECTION

Other Titles in This Collection

- *Marketing Your Value: 9 Steps to Navigate Your Career* by Michael Edmondson
- *Competencies at Work: Providing a Common Language for Talent Management* by Enrique Washington and Bruce Griffiths
- *Manage Your Career: 10 Keys to Survival and Success When Interviewing and on the Job, Second Edition* by Vijay Sathe
- *You're A Genius: Using Reflective Practice to Master the Craft of Leadership* by Steven S. Taylor
- *Major in Happiness: Debunking the College Major Fallacies* by Michael Edmondson
- *The Resilience Advantage: Stop Managing Stress and Find Your Resilience* by Richard S. Citrin and Alan Weiss
- *Success: Theory and Practice* by Michael Edmondson
- *Leading The Positive Organization: Actions, Tools, and Processes* by Thomas N. Duening
- *Performance Leadership™* by Karen Moustafa Leonard and Fatma Pakdil
- *The New Leader: Harnessing The Power of Creativity to Produce Change* by Renee Kosiarek

Announcing the Business Expert Press Digital Library

Concise e-books business students need for classroom and research

This book can also be purchased in an e-book collection by your library as

- *a one-time purchase,*
- *that is owned forever,*
- *allows for simultaneous readers,*
- *has no restrictions on printing, and*
- *can be downloaded as PDFs from within the library community.*

Our digital library collections are a great solution to beat the rising cost of textbooks. E-books can be loaded into their course management systems or onto student's e-book readers. The **Business Expert Press** digital libraries are very affordable, with no obligation to buy in future years. For more information, please visit **www.businessexpertpress.com/librarians.** To set up a trial in the United States, please contact **sales@businessexpertpress.com.**

www.ingramcontent.com/pod-product-compliance
Lightning Source LLC
Chambersburg PA
CBHW071837200326
41519CB00016B/4142